The Testaments
of the Twelve
Patriarchs

Guides to Apocrypha and Pseudepigrapha

Series Editor
Michael A. Knibb

THE TESTAMENTS OF THE TWELVE PATRIARCHS

Robert A. Kugler

Sheffield
Academic Press
www.SheffieldAcademicPress.com

Copyright © 2001 Sheffield Academic Press

Published by
Sheffield Academic Press Ltd
Mansion House
19 Kingfield Road
Sheffield S11 9AS
England

www.SheffieldAcademicPress.com

Typeset by Sheffield Academic Press
and
Printed on acid-free paper in Great Britain
by The Cromwell Press
Trowbridge, Wiltshire

British Library Cataloguing in Publication Data

A catalogue record for this book is available
from the British Library

ISBN 1 84127 193 4

Contents

Preface

The Guide demonstrates the distance a scholar can travel with time and maturity. My earlier work focused on the compositional history of Levi's testament and identified me with those who speculate on the shape of a pre-Christian form of the *Testaments* as a whole (*From Patriarch to Priest: The Levi-Priestly Tradition from Aramaic Levi to Testament of Levi* [SBLEJL, 9; Atlanta: Scholars Press, 1996a]). But as I did research for the Guide I grew more and more convinced of Marinus de Jonge's view of the matter, that there is no getting back to a pre-Christian *Testaments* (if there ever were one), and that we most profitably focus our attention on the Christian composition that remains to us. That bias comes through clearly in Chapter 1 of the Guide. There is too much still to discover by studying the *Testaments* as a Christian work to squander much effort on the search for 'origins'. This is not to deny that the *Testaments* preserve many Jewish exegetical motifs; indeed, revealing some of those is one focus of this Guide. It does mean, however, that we should no longer assume that the presence of Jewish interpretative material indicates a Jewish origin for the *Testaments*. Rather, it reveals the Christian authors' not-unexpected familiarity with those traditions, and appreciation of their power to appeal to Christian and Jewish audiences. Thus bringing out the relationships between the *Testaments*, the Hebrew Scriptures, and other Jewish exegetical traditions (as well as Graeco-Roman thought) is a substantial focus in Chapters 2 and 3 of the Guide.

Throughout the Guide quotations from the Greek text of the *Testaments* are taken from the *editio maior*, M. de Jonge *et al.*, *The Testaments of the Twelve Patriarchs: A Critical Edition of the Greek Text* (PsVTGr, I, 2; Leiden: E.J. Brill, 1978), and English quotations rely on H.W. Hollander and M. de Jonge, *The Testaments of the Twelve Patriarchs: A Commentary* (SVTP, 8; Leiden: E.J. Brill, 1985).

I owe a debt of thanks to a number of people. James VanderKam (University of Notre Dame) first directed me in my study of the Levi material and wisely guided my early explorations into the *Testaments*. And John Collins (University of Chicago) recommended me to Michael Knibb to compose this Guide. I can only hope that this small book honours Jim's guidance and John's confidence. In addition I extend a special word of gratitude to Michael Knibb. His patience permitted me the time to finish the Guide in the midst of teaching and family obligations, and his wisdom as an editor saved me from more than a few gaffes. Those that remain, of course, are entirely of my own making.

I dedicate this book to my wife who has, as scholars are wont to say of their spouses, more patience than I deserve. To her extraordinary credit, though, she also knows intuitively when to say 'Enough is enough'. As a result I not only know something of the *Testaments of the Twelve Patriarchs*—I also still know who my children and my wife are and that they are, at the end of the day, far more a joy to me than the sons of Jacob ever could be. So to you, reader, I commend the twelve patriarchs; for my part, it's time to take a trip to the park to play with my favourite people.

Abbreviations

AB	Anchor Bible
ABD	David Noel Freedman (ed.), *The Anchor Bible Dictionary* (New York: Doubleday, 1992)
ABRL	Anchor Bible Reference Library
AGJU	Arbeiten zur Geschichte des antiken Judentums und des Urchristentums
ALGHJ	Arbeiten zur Literatur und Geschichte des hellenistischen Judentums
ANRW	Hildegard Temporini and Wolfgang Haase (eds.), *Aufstieg und Niedergang der römischen Welt: Geschichte und Kultur Roms im Spiegel der neueren Forschung* (Berlin: W. de Gruyter, 1972–)
BETL	Bibliotheca ephemeridum theologicarum lovaniensum
BJS	Brown Judaic Studies
BZAW	Beihefte zur *ZAW*
CRINT	Compendia rerum iudaicarum ad Novum Testamentum
DJD	Discoveries in the Judaean Desert
EvT	*Evangelische Theologie*
ExpTim	*Expository Times*
HSM	Harvard Semitic Monographs
HTR	*Harvard Theological Review*
JBL	*Journal of Biblical Literature*
JJS	*Journal of Jewish Studies*
JQR	*Jewish Quarterly Review*
JSHRZ	Jüdische Schriften aus hellenistisch-römischer Zeit
JSJ	*Journal for the Study of Judaism in the Persian, Hellenistic and Roman Period*
JSP	*Journal for the Study of the Pseudepigrapha*
JTS	*Journal of Theological Studies*
LCL	Loeb Classical Library
NedTTs	*Nederlands theologisch tijdschrift*
NovT	*Novum Testamentum*
NTS	*New Testament Studies*
OBO	Orbis biblicus et orientalis
PsVTGr	Pseudepigrapha Veteris Testamenti Graece
RB	*Revue biblique*
RevQ	*Revue de Qumran*
RHPR	*Revue d'histoire et de philosophie religieuses*

SBLEJL	Society of Biblical Literature, Early Judaism and its Literature
SBLSCS	SBL Septuagint and Cognate Studies
SNT	Studien zum Neuen Testament
SPB	Studia postbiblica
SSN	Studia semitica neerlandica
ST	*Studia theologica*
STDJ	Studies on the Texts of the Desert of Judah
SHR	*Studies in the History of Religions*
SVTP	Studia in Veteris Testamenti pseudepigrapha
TS	*Theological Studies*
VC	*Vigiliae christianae*
VT	*Vetus Testamentum*
WMANT	Wissenschaftliche Monographien zum Alten und Neuen Testament
ZAW	*Zeitschrift für die alttestamentliche Wissenschaft*

1

AN INTRODUCTION TO THE TESTAMENTS OF THE TWELVE PATRIARCHS

The *Testaments of the Twelve Patriarchs* are the fictional valedictory speeches of the sons of Jacob. Completed sometime in the first two centuries of the Common Era, they consist of autobiography, exhortation and prediction. The *Testaments* provide rich evidence for understanding early Jewish and Christian thought. Yet few insights into Judaism and Christianity have been achieved from the *Testaments* because the battle over their parentage has so preoccupied those who investigate them. For example, some scholars resolve to study them exclusively as witnesses to early Christianity because they think it is impossible to get behind the present Christian form of the *Testaments*. Other scholars, noting that the *Testaments* incorporate traditional Jewish material, reconstruct the 'original *Testaments*' in order to cast light on early Judaism. And even though this second group of scholars has achieved no consensus on the scope of an original Jewish composition, they are nonetheless united in their rejection of the first group's notion that the *Testaments* may only be consulted for their witness to Christian thought. Thus the *Testaments* remain troubled orphans in the court of scholarly opinion, caught between the squabbling sponsors of their would-be parents.

Chapter 1 of this Guide surveys introductory issues associated with the *Testaments* and provides a brief recital of the long and contentious custody battle fought over them. This leads the Guide to the view that the surviving *Testaments* come from Christian authors, and that in spite of their obvious use of Jewish source materials, there is no hope of extracting from them an earlier Jewish work. Moreover, the Guide supports the view that the *Testaments'* authors aimed to instruct fellow Christians on proper conduct in God's sight and on the value of the patriarchs' teaching in that regard. The Guide's main interest, however, is not in rehearsing once more the elements of this sort of reading of the *Testaments*, although it does receive some attention. Rather, the Guide focuses chiefly on a neglected aspect of the *Testaments*, the possibility that Jews also encountered them in antiquity. The Guide asks what Jews would have experienced as a result of that encounter. It offers abundant evidence that Jewish recipients would have felt at home in the rhetorical world of the *Testaments*, and that they would have heard in them a proposal regarding God's abiding concern for their fate, one that argued for the coherence between their ancestors' instruction, the moral standards of the Graeco-Roman world in which they lived, and the redemptive power of Jesus and his teaching. They would have met in the *Testaments* an appeal to embrace the Christian option.

Contents

Although the waters navigated by the student of the *Testaments* can be treacherous, at least describing their contents provides relatively smooth sailing. No one denies that each speech conforms more or less to a well-defined pattern in which the patriarch recalls the past, instructs for the present, and predicts the future. Things become a bit trickier, however, when we draw conclusions about the *Testaments'* aim from the nature of their content. All the same, we may say this: even the mere rehearsal of the *Testaments'* contents reveals that their *effect* on ancient readers would have been to instruct Christians in proper conduct and argue that God's saving plans for the people of Israel were announced in their ancestors' words and fulfilled in Jesus.

Each testament begins with all or part of a standard introduction. It states that the testament is a copy of the patriarch's final words, announces the patriarch's impending death, gives his age at the time of death, and indicates that his family gathers around him on the occasion of his speech. Then the patriarch commands his audience to heed his instructions. Some testaments preserve other elements in the introduction, noting, for instance, that when he spoke the patriarch was well (*T. Levi* 1.2; *T. Naph.* 1.2; *T. Ash.* 1.2) or ill (*T. Reub.* 1.2; *T. Sim.* 1.2), that some of his brothers were also present (*T. Reub.* 1.4), or that the context of the testament was a banquet (*T. Naph.* 1.2).

The main body of each testament usually includes three parts: a biographical account (hagiography), moral exhortation supported by ethical discourse (ethics) and predictions of the future (eschatology). The amount of material devoted to each part is not consistent, but the general pattern does hold true in virtually all of the testaments.

The biographical accounts and the themes of the ethical sections are often linked to one another. And in all cases the patriarch urges his children to behave as he did or not, depending on his own past story. Doing 'the right thing' is identified throughout with pleasing God and fleeing from Beliar (Satan), and with keeping the twofold commandment to love God and one's neighbour. And as we will soon see, 'the right thing' is also implicitly identified with traditional Graeco-Roman standards of good conduct. So Reuben recalls his transgression with Bilhah (Gen. 35.22) and encourages his children to avoid the pitfalls of youthful foolishness, impurity and attachment to the beauty of women (*T. Reub.* 2.1–6.4). Simeon warns against the envy that led to his overweening desire to kill Joseph and his imprisonment in Egypt (Gen. 41.38; *T. Sim.* 2.2–5.3). Levi reminds his children of the zeal he had for the Lord (Gen. 34) and exhorts his descendants to observe the law with the same intensity (*T. Levi* 2.1–9.14; 11.1–13.9). Encouraging his children to be temperate and pure, Judah blames his sexual indiscretion (Gen. 38) on his love of money, impure desires and predilection for strong drink (*T. Jud.* 2.1–20.5). Issachar describes his life as a farmer (Gen. 49.14-15 LXX) and his concomitant life of 'simplicity'. Saying that virtue is the root of most other good character traits, Issachar commends it to his children (*T. Iss.* 1.2–5.3; 7.1-7). Zebulun describes his compassion for Joseph at the time of Joseph's sale and his own life as a 'simple' fisherman (Gen. 49.13 LXX) and encourages in his children a similar commitment to mercy and warm-heartedness (*T. Zeb.* 1.4–9.4). Like Simeon, Dan's envy engendered a desire to kill Joseph and led him to falsehood; thus he warns against jealousy and deceit (*T. Dan* 1.3–5.3). Because Naphtali found contentment in using his natural speed to serve as the family messenger, he encourages his children likewise to live in harmony with nature's order and goodness (*T. Naph.* 1.5–3.5; 8.4-10). Gad says that he became angry because Joseph's bad report to his father (Gen. 37.2a) was an inaccurate claim that the sons of Zilpah and Bilhah were eating the lambs of the flock; his rage produced a negative outcome for him and so he exhorts his children to control their tempers (*T. Gad* 1.2–7.7). Asher says that he sought single-mindedly to keep the law of God; around this he builds an explanation of double- and single-mindedness and an exhortation to choose the latter lifestyle (*T. Ash.* 1.3–6.6). Joseph recounts his difficulties with Potiphar's wife (Gen. 39.6b-18) and his self-restraint with respect to his brothers, even after they betrayed him (Gen. 50.20); he exhorts his listeners to live similar lives of prayer, chastity, endurance and care for others (*T. Jos.* 1.3–18.4). And Benjamin's brief biographical recollection focuses on Joseph and Joseph's explanation to Benjamin in Egypt of how he was sold to the Ishmaelites (Gen. 45.14-15), an explanation that excuses his brothers in the matter; thus, said Joseph, they should not be blamed. From this memory Benjamin launches into a panegyric for Joseph that describes him as a good man with a good mind, one whom Benjamin's children would do well to emulate (*T. Benj.* 1.2–8.3).

In the concluding eschatological sections the patriarchs predict their descendants' futures. Several sources provide the patriarchs with their information. Enoch is the most popular (*T. Sim.* 5.4; *T. Levi* 10.5; 14.1; 16.1; *T. Jud.* 18.1; *T. Naph.* 4.1; *T. Benj.* 9.1), but the fathers (*T. Levi* 10.1), the fathers' writings (*T. Zeb.* 9.5), and heavenly tablets (*T. Ash.* 7.5) are also cited. The future-oriented passages come in several different forms (de Jonge 1953). Sin–Exile–Return (S.E.R.) sections generally describe the future sins of the patriarch's descendants, the tribe's exile among the Gentiles as punishment for their sin, and God's restoration of the tribe. S.E.R. passages include *T. Levi* 10; 14–15; 16; *T. Jud.* 18.1; 23; *T. Iss.* 6; *T. Zeb.* 9.5-7, 9; *T. Dan* 5.4a, 6-9; *T. Naph.* 4.1-3, 5; *T. Gad* 8.2; *T. Ash.* 7.2-3, 5-7; *T. Benj.* 9.1-2; the testaments of Reuben, Simeon and Joseph lack S.E.R. passages. (For this list and further details regarding S.E.R. passages, see Hollander and de Jonge 1985: 39-41, 53-56.)

Levi–Judah (L.J.) passages are a second type of eschatological material. In some of these the patriarch bemoans his descendants' rebellion against Levi's and Judah's descendants (*T. Reub.* 6.5-7; *T. Sim.* 5.4-6), as well as their certain defeat in such efforts (cf. *T. Dan* 5.4; *T. Gad* 8.2). In others the patriarch looks forward to his descendants' loyalty and obedience to the tribes of Levi and Judah out of respect for their special roles in providing priests, kings, and, in time, the messiah of Israel. L.J. passages include *T. Reub.* 6.5–7.8, 10-12; *T. Levi* 2.11; *T. Sim.* 5.4-6; 7.1-2; *T. Jud.* 21.1-6a; *T. Iss.* 5.7-8; *T. Dan* 5.4, 6-7, 10; *T. Naph.* 8.2; *T. Gad* 8.1-2; *T. Jos.* 19.6; the testaments of Zebulun, Asher and Benjamin lack L.J. passages. (For this list and further details regarding L.J. passages, see Hollander and de Jonge 1985: 40-41, 56-61.)

The ideal saviour passages constitute a third type of future texts; they are closely related to the messianic L.J. passages (*T. Levi* 18; *T. Jud.* 24; *T. Zeb.* 9.8; *T. Dan* 5.10-13). *Testament of Levi* 18 anticipates a new high priest who will arise after the old priesthood has failed: he will exemplify all the best of the levitical line, be free from the taint of its corruption, and bring salvation to his people. *Testament of Judah* 24 looks forward to a redeemer king who will come from the line of Judah, although the existing lineage will first come to an end. *Testament of Zebulun* 9.8 describes a redeemer who will liberate those in captivity to Beliar. And *T. Dan* 5.10-13 anticipates a saviour from 'the tribe of Judah and Levi' who will also set free those in captivity to Beliar. Of course, all of these passages speak of Jesus.

A final group of future-oriented passages announce the resurrection of the patriarch to rule over his tribe at the second coming of the messiah (*T. Sim.* 6.7; *T. Levi* 18.14; *T. Jud.* 25; *T. Zeb.* 10.1-4; *T. Benj.* 10.6-10). These passages eventually include all of the patriarchs in the resurrection, along with Abraham, Isaac, and Jacob, Enoch, Noah and Shem, and all those whose observance of the law or embrace of Jesus as messiah made them righteous.

Altogether the future-oriented passages claim a number of things about what lies ahead for the patriarchs and for the early Common Era recipients of the *Testaments*. First, they predict the futures of the patriarchs' descendants—their successes and failures, righteousnesses and sins—up to the coming of Jesus. Second, they foretell the tribes' rebellion against the descendants of Levi (priests) and Judah (kings), and against the saviour who will come from those two tribes; at the same time they admonish obedience to the two tribes and to the messiah. Nonetheless, third, they predict that Israel, and most especially the tribe of Levi, will reject the messiah. After that, the messiah will turn away from Israel to the Gentiles, and Israel will sporadically keep the commandments in the period between the first advent of the messiah and his second coming. And fourth, the patriarchs announce that the messiah will come again to complete God's plan of salvation for Israel, to redeem those who have kept the law 'and/or believe[s] in Jesus Christ' (de Jonge 1986a: 210).

Each testament closes with all or some of the following elements: the patriarch says he has concluded his speech, gives instructions for the disposition of his remains, and dies. Lastly there is a report that his children followed his burial instructions.

It is hard not to see already how the *Testaments*, while clearly addressing issues associated with ethical conduct, by the very nature of their content also speak ably to Jews about God's concern for their fate in this world and the next. The patriarchs do propose patterns of conduct based on the twofold commandment to love God and one's neighbour, but they also admit that the tribes failed to heed their advice and paid the consequences for that failure in the past. They acknowledge in turn Israel's rejection of Jesus, whose own life and teaching confirmed the patriarchs' ethical instruction. And yet for all of that, they promise that the saviour will come again to offer yet another chance for Israel to embrace him and/or show its faith through the keeping of the commandments.

Genre

The ostensible genre of the *Testaments* is revealed by its title. Typically scholars define a testament, or 'farewell discourse', in one of two ways, by formal literary characteristics or by the nature of its content. There is wide agreement that a peculiar narrative framework constitutes a testament's formal literary characteristic. It includes an introduction in which the testator gathers family or friends to give his near-death speech, and a conclusion that narrates the speaker's death (Collins 1984: 325; see now also the classification 'Vermächtnisrede' from Winter 1994). Meanwhile, no such consensus exists among those who determine testaments by their content. For some, the *sine qua non* is parenesis (Baltzer 1960; von Nordheim 1980); others insist that speeches forecasting the future or apocalyptic in outlook typify the genre (Munck 1950); and still others say that testaments merge parenesis and apocalyptic (e.g., *Testament of Levi*; see Kolenkow 1975). Given this lack of consensus, it seems best to admit that content alone cannot determine the genre. Thus only the narrative framework remains as its distinguishing characteristic. By this measure the speeches of all twelve patriarchs easily qualify as 'testaments' or 'farewell discourses'.

Jews and Christians would certainly have recognized this genre. After all, the *Testaments* are modelled in large part on the biblical farewell discourses of such figures as Jacob (Gen. 49), Moses (Deut. 33), and David (1 Chron. 28–29), to name but a few (for a proponent of this view, see Cortès 1976). Given their experience with those speeches, the audience would have expected the patriarchs' accurate, if only rather general, prediction of the ancestors' future and their own past (see, for example, Jacob on Judah in Gen. 49.8-12; or Moses on Levi in Deut. 33.8-11). And that is exactly what they received. For example, in *T. Jud.* 21.7–22.1 Judah unerringly foretells his descendants' failure at kingship and *T. Levi* 16.3 foretokens priestly complicity in Jesus' death.

However, the *Testaments* move somewhat beyond the boundaries of the farewell discourse in that they predict not only the speakers' future and the recipients' past; they also announce the recipients' future by promising Jesus' second coming, at which time all who embrace him will be redeemed (e.g., *T. Levi* 16.5; *T. Ash.* 7.7). Thus by revealing the secrets of a time yet to come the speeches become 'apocalyptic' farewell discourses that encourage acceptance of Jesus as a redeemer. In this way even the *Testaments'* genre assists in asserting God's abiding interest in Israel's salvation.

Main Themes

By most accounts ethics are the *Testaments'* central theme. After all, almost without exception the patriarchs' autobiographical comments lay the groundwork for moral exhortation, and the consequences of heeding the fathers' exhortation or ignoring it appear to be the centre of concern in the eschatological sections. While this is true, a closer look suggests that theology might have been the *Testaments'* unifying theme for those who experienced them in antiquity. As we shall see, the *Testaments* work in the following manner. First, patriarchal moral instruction is implicitly identified with Hellenistic (and Hellenistic-Jewish and Christian) ethical norms; thus the *Testaments* equate a successful lifestyle in the Graeco-Roman world with conduct defined by the ancestors as pleasing to God. Second, the *Testaments* assert an equivalency between the ancestors' teaching (Graeco-Roman standards of conduct) and the keeping of God's twofold commandment to love God and neighbour. Third, they hold up Joseph as proof that one can heed the fathers' instructions and fulfil the double commandment. And fourth, they make Joseph into a type of Jesus. So, taken altogether, the *Testaments'* moral instructions lead inexorably to the insight that leading life well in the Graeco-Roman world is not only God-pleasing; it is also an expression of one's consent to God's roadmap toward salvation given through the instruction of the patriarchs, the twofold law given through Moses, and the teachings and life of Jesus. Thus the ethical discourse of the *Testaments* would, in the end, also have been experienced as a proposal regarding God's plan for God's people.

The ancestors' ethical teachings undeniably echo broadly defined popular Hellenistic, Christian and Jewish teaching on virtues and vices (see, for example, H.W. Hollander 1981; Kee 1978; de Jonge 1985b, 1989a, 1989b, 1990). Sexual restraint stands at the heart of Reuben's, Judah's, Issachar's and Joseph's biographical accounts. Envy occupies Simeon's attention. The problem of arrogance constitutes a focus of Levi's discourse. Valour finds a place in Judah's autobiographical recollections, but lust and greed becloud his reputation. Compassion and mercy characterize Zebulun. Anger and hatred consume Dan and Gad. Coherence with the natural order gives Naphtali a topic to address. And often the foundational Hellenistic virtue ἁπλότης, 'simplicity', and vice πορνεία, 'impurity', function as the overarching themes of a patriarch's ethical address.

Specific ties to Graeco-Roman, Christian, and Hellenistic-Jewish texts are abundant as well. So *T. Jud.* 18.4 reflects Eccl. 4.8 LXX, on the negative power of πορνεία and φιλαργυρία, 'love of money' (Hollander and de Jonge 1985: 217). Concern for the weak and needy in Job 30.25; 31.17,

39 LXX is taken up in *T. Iss.* 7.5 (Hollander and de Jonge 1985: 251). And the claim in *T. Naph.* 2.3 that God measured precisely all of creation's works echoes *Wis.* 11.20 (Hollander and de Jonge 1985: 303). Rachel's ἐγκράτεια, 'self-control', regarding sexual intercourse in the *Testament of Issachar* parallels the standard Graeco-Roman, Christian and Hellenistic-Jewish view on marital relations (see Musonius *Fragments* 13A-B [Lutz]; Philo, *Op. Mund.* 161; *Abr.* 137, 248-49 [Colson *et al.*]; Justin, *Apology* 1.29 [Falls]; cf. de Jonge 1990). The encompassing virtue of ἁπλότης, 'simplicity', is preached by all three traditions (Amstutz 1968). Reuben's use of συνείδησις, 'conscience', in *T. Reub.* 4.3 matches the common Hellenistic, Christian and Hellenistic-Jewish notion of conscience (*Wis.* 17.10; Josephus, *Ant.* 2.52 [Thackeray *et al.*]; Hollander and de Jonge 1985: 100). And the list could go on.

The *Testaments* also say that heeding the patriarchs' advice fulfils the double command to love God and neighbour (Deut. 6.5; Lev. 19.18). It is true that the law takes a back seat to more general standards, that 'the *Testaments* nowhere teach the observance of the Sabbath, or of circumcision, or of the dietary laws' (de Jonge 1985b: 169; see, however, the claims of Slingerland 1986, and the reply of de Jonge 1989a: 549-50; note also my comments on provenance below at the end of the section on 'Provenance, Date, Compositional History and Purpose'). Nevertheless, they do regularly integrate heeding the patriarchs' instructions with the fulfilment of the double commandment to love God (Deut. 6.5) and neighbour (Lev. 19.18). The twofold commandment appears clearly for the first time as the key to a virtuous life in *T. Iss.* 5.2; 7.6-7; and again in *T. Dan* 5.2-3; *T. Gad* 4.1-2; *T. Jos.* 11.1; *T. Benj.* 3.1-3. But well before that point in the *Testaments*, and after it, the double commandment makes furtive appearances in the narrative that function in the same way. For example, in *T. Reub.* 6.8-9 the patriarch urges his descendants to obey Levi in cultic matters—that is, give God honour through sacrifice—and to 'do truth each one to his neighbour'. Likewise, in *T. Sim.* 5.2 the ancestor says, 'make your hearts good before the Lord and make your ways straight before men'. In both cases, fulfilment of the double commandment is equated with satisfying the patriarchs' demands.

Joseph's life and conduct prove that the *Testaments*' ethics can be accomplished, lest the reader despair of achieving those norms. All of the testaments, save those of Issachar and Asher, recall Joseph's virtuous conduct. They recount how he exercised sexual self-restraint, maintained his emotional equilibrium in the midst of triumph and tribulation, exercised compassion and mercy even for his enemies, was without envy, and did not get violently angry at others even when he had reason to be enraged (see the further discussion of Joseph below and the treatment of him in the other testaments in Chapter 2). And the final testament, that of Benjamin, eulogizes Joseph as the quintessential 'good man' with a 'good mind' who achieved what the patriarchs asked, what Graeco-Roman society requests of its citizens, and what God's twofold commandment demands.

Not only this, the *Testaments* also make Joseph a type of Jesus (*T. Zeb.* 2.2; 3.3; *T. Gad* 2.3; *T. Benj.* 3.8). In doing this they identify his conduct with that of Jesus, who after all is called a 'renewer of the law' (*T. Levi* 16.3), and whose life is thought by the *Testaments* to be not only redemptive for those who believe in him, but also exemplary to all those who wish to keep the commandments.

The effect of these emphases, as indicated above, is to render the *Testaments'* ethical agenda a theological proposal. By counselling through the patriarchs' speeches a virtuous life according to Graeco-Roman standards, by identifying that with the fulfilment of God's commandments, and by acclaiming Joseph as proof that it may be done and making him a type of Jesus, the *Testaments* impressed upon their recipients God's merciful and even relentless provision of multiple paths to salvation.

The sections of the *Testaments* devoted to the second theme, eschatology, underscore this view of the relationship between ethics and theology. The patriarchs' future predictions prove that when the tribes heed their forefathers' advice they fare well (*T. Sim.* 6.2-4); but when they ignore the patriarch's instructions (or when they rebel against Levi and Judah) they are punished (*T. Sim.* 5.4-6). Doing well, say the ethical sections and the future predictions, depends on fleeing Beliar to live under God's care (*T. Sim.* 2.4-6). Conversely, those who remain subject to the sway of Beliar and his evil spirits also remain under the spell of their vices (*T. Iss.* 6.1). It would seem, then, that all depends on doing the right thing through God's guidance and escape from the Evil One. Yet even here the focus on ethics gives way to a theological assertion. For the patriarchs predict, almost without exception, that their descendants will fail to heed their advice; the tribes will accede to Beliar's influence. The ethical counsel of the patriarchs seems to have been entirely for naught, and the tribes appear doomed. But it is not to remain so. For next the patriarchs predict God's intervention through a saviour who will secure Israel's fate by destroying the power of Beliar and his spirits (*T. Levi* 18.12; *T. Jud.* 25.3; *T. Zeb.* 9.8; *T. Dan* 5.10-11), and by offering salvation at his second coming even to those who fail utterly to attain virtue (*T. Levi* 16.5; *T. Ash.* 7.7). Thus, just as ethics give way to theology, a transcendent theme of the *Testaments'* preoccupation with the future is the further revelation of God's unrelenting grace for those who show their trust by deed or faith.

Main Figures

Three patriarchs, Levi, Judah and Joseph, feature as central characters in the *Testaments*. Their treatment in the *Testaments* also underscores the view that the work not only provides ethical instruction to Christians, but also offers a way for Jews into the Christian community of faith.

The patriarchs frequently refer to Levi and Judah in the future-oriented sections to imbue the promised saviour with priestly and royal characteristics, traits that would make him attractive to Jewish audiences. True, Levi and Judah, the progenitors of priesthood and kingship in Israel, figure quite naturally in the future-oriented speeches of the other patriarchs: the patriarchs foretell the rise and eventual corruption of the priesthood and monarchy through the misdeeds of Levi's and Judah's descendants (*T. Levi* 10; 14–16; *T. Jud.* 21.7–22.1; *T. Dan* 5.7), and, not surprisingly, they instruct their children to obey Levi's and Judah's priestly and royal descendants (*T. Iss.* 5.7-8). But more frequently the patriarchs mention Levi and Judah in order to predict a saviour who would function in the roles associated with the two lines, as king over all (Judah) and as priestly mediator between God and humanity (Levi) (*T. Sim.* 7.1-2; *T. Levi* 2.11; *T. Jos.* 19.6). After all, these were essential attributes for a messiah who would appeal to the turn-of-the-era Jewish imagination. The patriarchs also refer to the deliverer to warn that many of their descendants, even those of Levi and Judah, would deny him when he appears (*T. Levi* 4.4). Nonetheless, say the patriarchs, this same priestly and royal figure will return and mercifully offer a second chance for the sake of Abraham, Isaac and Jacob (*T. Levi* 15.4; 16.5; *T. Ash.* 7.7).

Meanwhile, Joseph is a key figure in the *Testaments'* ethical speculation and biographical accounts (for a complete treatment of Joseph as the 'ethical model' in the *Testaments*, see H.W. Hollander 1981; note as well the use of the date of his death as the measure in time of some of his brothers' deaths; *T. Reub.* 1.2; *T. Sim.* 1.1). In every testament except those assigned to Issachar and Asher he is the paradigmatic 'good man' (for example, *T. Benj.* 3–8), and in many he is also the victim whose ill-fortune elucidates another patriarch's vice (for example, *T. Zeb.* 8.4-5). His experience proves that one can accomplish what the patriarchs ask, and that, while one may suffer some difficulties for good behaviour (*T. Gad* 2.1-5), the persistently virtuous will be rewarded (*T. Levi* 13.9). He also proves that virtue comes precisely from dependence on the God of Israel and the keeping of God's double commandment (*T. Benj.* 3.1-4). In addition, Joseph's identification with Jesus (see, for example, *T. Zeb.* 2.2; 3.3; *T. Gad* 2.3; *T. Benj.* 3.8; on the identification of Joseph with

Jesus in early Christian literature, see Argyle 1955–56) indicates the coherence of virtuous conduct, as it is defined by the patriarchs, with the teachings and actions of Jesus. Thus Joseph not only serves as a model of virtuous behaviour for Christian and Jewish readers, he also provides further encouragement to Jewish recipients of the *Testaments* to embrace Jesus as saviour.

Relationship with Early Jewish and Christian Texts and Traditions and Hellenistic Thought and Literature

Connections among the *Testaments* and the forms, content and thought of Jewish, Christian and Hellenistic texts are numerous. While the links have engendered hope that by their comparative use one might determine the date and provenance of the *Testaments* (see Macky 1969), little has come of such effort. But noting the links does bear fruit for our interest in determining how the *Testaments* might have been received by Christians and Jews. Indeed, the strongest connections turn out to be with texts and traditions that are useful in instructing Christians in ethical conduct and arguing that Jews should embrace Jesus as saviour.

As we have already seen, the *Testaments* rely on the farewell discourse genre set forth in Gen. 49 and Deut. 33, but they also give it an apocalyptic emphasis by predicting their recipients' future. It is a genre that Christians and Jews would have easily recognized and appreciated. Moreover, we know that the genre would have developed in its recipients the expectation of reliable prophecy from the speakers, preparing them to receive the prophecy of their own potential fate. (It is worth noting, as an aside, that at least in a formal way the *Testaments* are also comparable to other non-biblical farewell discourses from the period. Certainly the *Testament of Job* and probably the *Testament of Moses* share the distinctive narrative framework, although the contents of the latter two works differ substantially from those of the *Testaments*. See also 4Q Visions of Amram[a-f] ['A copy of the writing of the words of the visions of Amram', 4Q543 1 1]; 4Q Testament of Kohath [4Q542; Vermes].) The *Testaments* and the apocalyptic genre compare most favourably precisely at this point. True, at a purely formal level the *Testaments* and apocalyptic texts share little in common, and only *T. Levi* 2–5 provides a full-blown apocalyptic passage. But the use of *vaticinia ex eventu* to establish a seer's credibility as he predicts the recipients' real future *is* a critical element common to historical apocalypses and the *Testaments*.

As a genre, the *Testaments* have also been compared with the 'covenant formulary', a speech that states covenantal obligations and motivates the audience to keep them either by a rehearsal of God's wondrous deeds in history or through blessings and curses (cf. Dan. 9; Neh. 9; Bar. 1.5–3.8; 3 Macc. 2.2-20; Tob. 3.1-6; Baltzer 1960). However, the actual ebb and flow of the *Testaments'* narrative limits the usefulness of this comparison, and the exhortations in the *Testaments* lack the association with the law that would make such a comparison effective.

The biographical sections make wide use of simple prose narrative accounts. But a great variety of other sub-genres appear as well. There are synagogue homilies (*T. Jud.* 13–17), hymns (*T. Sim.* 6.2-7), visions (*T. Levi* 2.5–5.7; *T. Naph.* 5–6; 7), prayers (*T. Levi* 4.2), instructions (*T. Levi* 9), battle accounts (*T. Jud.* 3–7), seriatim memoirs (*T. Levi* 11; *T. Jud.* 2), paronomasia (*T. Iss.* 1.3-15; *T. Zeb.* 1.2-3), aetiologies (*T. Zeb.* 6.1-3), and Rewritten Bible texts (*T. Levi* 6.3–7.4; *T. Jos.* 3.1–9.5; 11.2–16.6). The Hebrew and Greek scriptures provide all of these genres, but many also appear in the wider Jewish, Christian and Hellenistic literature at the turn of the era. Thus they would have been easily recognized by Jews and Christians of the era and would have made the *Testaments* readily comprehensible to those encountering them.

A narrower range of sub-genres appears within the parenetical sections of the *Testaments*. Aschermann (1955) identified various forms of exhortation (for a listing, see H.W. Hollander 1981: 11) and traced them back mostly to the wisdom books of the Septuagint. Hollander adds that 'non-Jewish Hellenistic authors' such as Musonius (first century CE) used many of the same forms. Likewise, the popular-philosophic diatribe, known from the time of Teles (third century BCE) on, regularly turns up in the *Testaments'* hortatory sections as well (H.W. Hollander 1981: 12). These forms, too, would have made Christians and Jews living in the Hellenistic world feel at home in the rhetorical world of the *Testaments*.

Marinus de Jonge already classified the sub-genres within the future-oriented sections of the Testaments in 1953. De Jonge's 'S.E.R.', 'L.J.', 'ideal saviour', and 'resurrection of the patriarch' genre titles, however, do little to locate the material in relationship to other genres of the period. It is true that the S.E.R. form affiliates well with Deuteronomic recitations of history (Steck 1967), but there are better parallels in Old Testament prophetic literature. The S.E.R. passages and the L.J. passages that predict rebellion against the tribes of Levi and Judah echo prophetic oracles of indictment and judgment (Amos 7.16-17). The L.J. passages that promote loyalty and obedience to the tribes of Levi and Judah recall the admonitory speeches of the prophets (Jer. 25.3-6). And the ideal saviour, resurrection of the patriarch, and messianic L.J. passages resonate with promises of salvation (Isa. 41.8-13) and announcements of deliverers (Jer. 23.1-8). Significantly, by the first century CE prophetic texts had come to have real predictive power among Jewish readers (Barton 1986: 179-234).

So Jewish readers especially would not only have been comfortable with these forms: they would have been encouraged by them to accept the predictive speech of the patriarchs as accurate.

The contents of the *Testaments* also resonate with a great body of Hellenistic and early Jewish and Christian literature in ways that help the *Testaments* appeal to a Christian and Jewish audience. First, it is widely agreed that they rely heavily on the rhetoric, content and thought of the Septuagint, the authoritative scriptures for many Christians and Jews of the era. For instance, the *Testaments'* explanations of the names of the patriarchs and/or professions depend often on the Septuagint (see, for example, *T. Jud.* 1.3; *T. Iss.* 1.15; *T. Zeb.* 1.3; *T. Naph.* 1.6; *T. Benj.* 1.6). Connections between the hortatory sections in the *Testaments* and the wisdom and psalms of the Septuagint are well documented (H.W. Hollander 1981; Küchler 1979; von Nordheim 1980; cf. *T. Jud.* 18.4 and Eccl. 4.8; *T. Iss.* 7.5 and Job 31.17, 39; *T. Naph.* 2.3 and Wis. 11.20). But perhaps the best evidence of the confluence between the Septuagint and the *Testaments* is their shared rhetoric. As Chapter 3 will show, the common rhetoric probably evoked in recipients not just reminiscences of the Septuagint's language, but of its story-world and ethos as well. This too is important for understanding how the *Testaments* appealed not only to Christians, but also to Jews.

Fragments of Jewish pseudepigrapha and rabbinic folklore also turn up in the *Testaments*, especially in the biographical sections; these 'exegetical motifs' (Kugel 1997, 1998) were also surely significant in making the *Testaments* accessible to Jewish recipients. A few examples must suffice. The accounts of Reuben's sin with Bilhah in *T. Reub.* 3.9–4.5 and *Jub.* 33.9-20 share more in common with one another than they do with the brief biblical reference to the encounter (Gen. 35.22). The two-mandrakes-for-sex story in *T. Iss.* 1.3–2.5 has a particularly interesting parallel in *Gen. Rab.* 72.3, 5 (Neusner; see Chapter 2 below). The unusual link between Zebulun and the sailor's life (*T. Zeb.* 6.1-7) also turns up in *Gen. Rab.* 72.5; 98.12; 99.9 (Neusner). The stories of Judah's war with the Amorites and his conflict with Esau appear in *T. Jud.* 3–7; 9 and again in *Jub.* 34.1-9; 37.1–38.14 (and later in expanded form in *Midrash Wayissa'u* [=*Chronicle of Yerahmeel* 36-37] and the *Book of Yashar*; VanderKam 1977: 218-19 n. 23; Hollander and de Jonge 1985: 26, 451-56). The visions in *T. Naph.* 5–7 reappear in the Hebrew *T. Naph.* 2–6 (see below). And Dan is treated with disdain in the targumic tradition much as he is in the *Testaments* (*Targ. Ps.-J.* Deut. 25.18 [Clarke]).

Given their Christian authorship, the *Testaments'* connections to the New Testament's content and thought are hardly surprising (for lists of related passages, see, among others, Argyle 1952; Charles 1908b). Again, a few examples will have to suffice. The notion in *T. Jos.* 19.3 that a virgin from Judah will bear a lamb without fault recalls the Matthaean and Lukan birth narratives (compare Justin, *Apology* 1.32 [Falls; Hollander and de Jonge 1985: 408]). *Testament of Judah* 24.1-2 and Mt. 3.16; Mk 1.10 speak of a messiah who will see the heavens open over him. And *T. Reub.* 5.5 and 1 Cor. 6.18a share some striking rhetoric (see Chapter 2 below).

Elements of the thought world and literature of the early Christian church also mirror themes in the *Testaments*. While there are many, small parallels between the *Testaments* and early Christian thought (see Hollander and de Jonge 1985: 67-82; de Jonge 1985a; and in general, de Jonge 1991a), two large-scale points of comparison require attention as further evidence that the *Testaments* constitute an effort to educate Christians on proper conduct but could also be read by Jews as encouragement to embrace Jesus as saviour. First, the ethics of the *Testaments* compare very favourably with those of a number of other Christian didactic works (the *Didache*, the *Epistle of Barnabas*, and the *Shepherd of Hermas*; de Jonge 1953: 119-20; but see Collins 1984: 341, who warns that these commonalities may result from common dependence on the general ethic of Hellenistic Judaism). Yet, second, de Jonge has pointed out a comparison that is highly suggestive regarding the *Testaments'* possible function in relationship to a Jewish audience: they resemble the works of 'early Christian writers like Justin, Irenaeus, Melito, [and] Hippolytus' (de Jonge 1989b: 205; see also de Jonge 1985a, 1985b), authors who held the view that people can become God's own apart from the law of Moses, through observing the patriarchs' double command to love God and one's neighbour, a double command that they also equate with the teaching of Jesus (see de Jonge 1985b).

Finally, we note the connections between the *Testaments* and popular Graeco-Roman philosophy. These links pervade the *Testaments* and indicate how they identify a properly pious way of life with standards of conduct equally acceptable to their recipients' Graeco-Roman neighbours and overlords. Kee has devoted attention to the connections between the *Testaments* and Cynic–Stoic philosophy (1978), and H.W. Hollander (1981) adds still more on this. For example, in addressing the reasons for Reuben's lustful behaviour *T. Reub.* 2.3-8 takes up the Stoic notions of motivating forces for human action (Aetius 4.21.1-4 [Long and Sedley 1987: 315-16] Philo, *Quaest. in Gen.* 1.75 [Colson *et al.*]; Kee 1978: 266). Envy (φθόνος), the central theme of *T. Sim.* 2.6–5.3, is a popular *topos* among the classical moralists, especially Plutarch (see Chapters 2 and 3). According to much Cynic and Stoic thought Issachar's virtue of 'simplicity' (ἁπλότης) lays the necessary foundation for the achievement of other virtues promoted by the Graeco-Roman philosophical imagination.

Rachel's 'continency' (ἐγκρατεία) in *T. Iss.* 1.3–2.5 is the heart of the Graeco-Roman sexual ethic. And Benjamin's depiction of Joseph as the 'good man' takes up another common Hellenistic *topos* (for a more complete listing of the themes shared by *Testaments* and Cynic and Stoic philosophy, see Kee 1978).

The foregoing survey of links between the *Testaments* and other Christian, Hellenistic and Jewish literature proves the authors' wide familiarity with this literature. But even more so, it shows that the *Testaments'* authors used genres, content and rhetoric that Christian *and* Jewish audiences would have easily recognized and appreciated.

By way of addendum, it is necessary to devote attention to one connection that is often suggested, but must be rejected. Supposed links between the sectarian literature of Qumran and the *Testaments* captured scholarly attention almost immediately after the discovery of the Dead Sea Scrolls (Dupont-Sommer 1953; Philonenko 1960). To name only two of the links, investigators noted the shared use of the name 'Beliar' for the chief agent of evil, and they read the scrolls and the *Testaments* as promoting the idea of two messiahs, one of priestly lineage and one of royal descent. Yet other works also use the name Beliar, and a close look at the *Testaments'* messianism reveals that they do not anticipate two messiahs, but only one with the characteristics of the tribes of Levi and Judah (see de Jonge 1986b). Furthermore, for each of these supposed parallels even more substantial differences between the *Testaments* and the scrolls come to mind. For example, the *Testaments* show none of the scrolls' intense interest in purity, the scrolls are preoccupied with community organization and governance, a theme completely absent from the *Testaments*, and the *Testaments* show almost no overt interest in Mosaic law, while the scrolls passionately interpret and promote the keeping of the law.

Textual Witnesses

The number and general character of the textual witnesses to the *Testaments of the Twelve Patriarchs* are well known, and, in spite of efforts to the contrary, they have not helped to establish a pre-Christian form of the *Testaments*.

There are fourteen Greek manuscripts dating from the tenth to the eighteenth centuries CE. Most divide into two families, while some can only be classified as individual manuscripts. Manuscripts *bk* make up family I and most of the rest constitute family II, which further divide into subfamilies according to their distinctive variants. H.J. de Jonge's analysis of the manuscripts shows that the differences between the two families indicate that the *Testaments* were transliterated twice from majuscule to minuscule writing. The archetype of the surviving textual tradition was a manuscript in uncial script earlier than the ninth century. Thus manuscript *b* represents the oldest available witness (*k* is excluded because it is too fragmentary), and its comparison with texts from family II permit the critical reconstruction of the archetype (H.J. de Jonge 1975a).

There are Armenian, Slavonic, Serbian and Latin versions of the *Testaments*. All but the Latin, which is Robert Grosseteste's 1242 translation from the Greek manuscript *b*, belong to family II (on Grosseteste, see de Jonge 1991b). The New Greek (eighteenth century) and the Serbian (sixteenth century) versions have no text-critical value. Although Charles used it to construct his critical edition (Charles 1908a), the Slavonic (eleventh century) is also now recognized to lack text-critical value (Turdeanu 1970; Gaylord and Korteweg 1975). Only the Armenian version continues to play a role in reconstructing an archetype, yet even here scholars differ over how much it should be used. De Jonge's *editio maior* uses it only to improve Greek readings seven times (de Jonge *et al.* 1978: 192-93); in general the Leiden school holds the Armenian version in low regard for text-critical purposes. Meanwhile, A. Hultgård treats it as a slightly more reliable witness (Hultgård 1982), but, as de Jonge has often pointed out (see most recently 1993: 10), Hultgård's text-critical method is open to serious question and his use of the Armenian may not be trusted. M. Stone, on the other hand, suggests on the basis of his careful study of a late tenth-century Armenian manuscript which contains extracts from the *Testaments* that an Armenian translation may have been made as early as the fifth or sixth century (Stone 1991: 152-53). In support of this claim Stone cites in particular the absence of vocabulary typical of a 'Philo-Hellene school' that affected the Armenian language in the late fifth and early sixth centuries (152). But de Jonge cautions against taking Stone's conclusions too seriously for text-critical purposes, saying that 'arguments on the strength of vocabulary or style are tenuous, because this kind of narrative and exhortative literature...has its own peculiar style and vocabulary' (1993: 11). He rightly counsels that we wait for 'unequivocal quotations from or allusions to the Testaments in the writings of early Armenian authors' before accepting Stone's judgments (11). (Also on the Armenian, see Burchard 1969, who argues that one can build from the Armenian manuscripts an eclectic text datable to the sixth or seventh century; as such it does not provide a witness better than the Greek, but it is 'older and more certain' than the Greek manuscripts [28].)

Seeking evidence of a still older textual witness among the quotations of the *Testaments* in the works of early Christian writers is disappointing. The earliest references (Origen, *Homilies on Joshua* 15.6 [Bruce]; Jerome, *Homilies on the Psalms* 61 [Ps. 15] [Ewald]) are too brief and too few to provide any insight into the nature of the texts used by early Christian writers.

Given these facts, Marinus de Jonge and his Leiden colleagues have concluded that the earliest attainable text of the *Testaments* is little younger than the ninth century CE. They reject the notion that textual criticism of the *Testaments* provides insight into their compositional history, much less abets the search for a pre-Christian, Jewish form of the work. One can say little against this view. (Likewise, one does well to trust the *editio maior* produced by the Leiden school; thus all Greek quotations of the *Testaments* in this volume are taken from de Jonge *et al.* 1978. English quotations, unless noted otherwise, are from the translation prepared from the *editio maior*, Hollander and de Jonge 1985.)

In spite of the Leiden school's warnings, some still try to argue from the differences among the Greek witnesses and the versions (especially the Armenian) that the *Testaments* were once a Jewish work, and that toying with the versions provides a glimpse of that text's form. In 1893 F.C. Conybeare wrote that the relative absence of 'Christian' passages in the Armenian indicates that it relied on a Greek textual tradition which was older than the one preserved in the extant manuscripts, a tradition that more closely reflects a Jewish original of the *Testaments*. R.H. Charles incorporated Conybeare's views in his stemma of the Greek manuscripts to posit two traditions that he traced back to two different Hebrew recensions. On that basis, and with the help of the Slavonic version, Charles claimed he was able to isolate the Christian interpolations into a Jewish text of the *Testaments* that dated from the days of John Hyrcanus (Charles 1908a, 1908b). J.W. Hunkin (1914) and N. Messel (1918) challenged Charles' text-critical methods and judgments and suggested that a more judicious approach showed the longer, 'Christian' Greek manuscripts to be the oldest and most reliable witnesses to the *Testaments*. Then Stone's work on the Armenian version demonstrated that the minuses are more probably the result of a translator's increasing sloth as he progressed in his task; indeed, the further one reads into the text, the more numerous are the minuses (Stone 1969). Consequently most agree that the Armenian and Slavonic versions in family II add little to our understanding of the earliest text of the *Testaments*, and certainly do not assist in the reconstruction of a pre-Christian Jewish *Vorlage*.

Related to the matter of textual witnesses is the debate regarding the *Testaments*' original language. Charles argued that the *Testaments* must go back to an original Hebrew. He insisted that the two text families which he identified in his stemma were based on two different Hebrew recensions (Charles 1908a, 1908b). However, the stemma and textual history worked out by the Leiden group invalidate Charles' stemma and concomitant claim regarding the *Testaments*' original language. Still, Anders Hultgård suggested that the *Testaments* were composed first in Aramaic and only later translated into Greek. He points to what he says are Semitisms outside of the portions of the *Testaments* known to be related to Aramaic or Hebrew source material (Hultgård 1982: 164-87). However, as Hollander and de Jonge (1985: 28) note, there are serious difficulties with Hultgård's claim. Many of the Greek words or phrases he identifies probably derive their semitic flavour from reliance on the Septuagint (compare *T. Jud.* 24.1 and Num. 24.17 LXX), large portions of the *Testaments* lack any hint of Hultgård's 'semitic flavour', and much of the *Testaments*' vocabulary comes from Greek Stoic writings and from the wisdom books of the Septuagint for which there were no Hebrew originals (Kee 1978). Clearly the evidence weighs heavily in favour of the view that the *Testaments* were composed in Greek.

Source Documents

Several fragmentary Jewish works provide what appear at first to be source materials for the *Testaments of the Twelve Patriarchs*, texts that might be helpful in reconstructing a Jewish, pre-Christian, form of the *Testaments*. Yet for all the hope they inspired in that regard, close examination of these texts usually reveals only a distant relationship, and in no case is there anything valuable for fully reconstructing an immediately prior form of the *Testaments*. These texts do, however, provide another indication of how Jewish recipients of the *Testaments* would have encountered in them comfortable and familiar territory.

Parallels to the *Testament of Naphtali* come from several different sources. The Hebrew *Testament of Naphtali*, attested in two recensions, has long been known (Gaster 1894). Like the *Testament of Naphtali* it gives two visions (*T. Naph.* 5–7; *T. Naph.* 2–6 [MT]) and a description of the human body's organization as evidence of God's ordered creation (*T. Naph.* 2.8; *T. Naph.* 10.5-7 [MT]). Some think that the *Hebrew Testament of Naphtali* is later than the *Testament of Naphtali*, and in certain places, a reworking of the Greek text (Schnapp 1884; Becker 1970; Hultgård 1982: 128-35). Others think that the Hebrew *Testament of Naphtali* is an earlier source for the Greek testament or that the two relied on an earlier common source (Charles 1908b; Gaster 1894; de Jonge 1953; Korteweg 1975).

Another possible source for the *Testament of Naphtali* is a small manuscript from Qumran, 4Q215. This is a late Hasmonean Hebrew manuscript (although, thanks to a 'mélecture onomastique', Milik thinks it was translated from Aramaic [1978: 97]), which J.T. Milik dubbed 4QT(estament) N(aphtali) because frg. 1.2-5 parallels *T. Naph.* 1.11-12, Bilhah's birth and genealogy (see now DJD 22: 73-82; Nebe 1994). Together the surviving fragments of 4Q215 and the two recensions of Hebrew *Testament of Naphtali* fail to provide any convincing evidence that a full-blown testament of Naphtali existed prior to the composition of the Greek *Testaments*, and virtually no one makes that claim. While the Qumran text may reflect a source, or better, a tradition used in the *Testaments*, and the Hebrew *Testament of Naphtali* material could be understood in the same way, both lack the characteristic narrative framework of a testament and do not otherwise parallel the *Testament of Naphtali*.

Equally unconvincing as evidence of a pre-Christian form of an individual testament is the material associated with *T. Jud.* 3–7. *Midrash Wayissa'u* (cf. the parallel in the late *Chronicle of Yerahmeel*) provides an account of the war against the Amorites similar to that given in *T. Jud.* 3–7 and recounted in much briefer form in *Jub.* 34.1-9. While it has been suggested that there was an oral tradition to which all of these relate (Becker 1970) or that *T. Jud.* 3–7 is an abbreviation of a longer version which was the source for *Midrash Wayissa'u*, de Jonge's view that we cannot be certain on any account about the relationships among the witnesses should be accepted (de Jonge 1953). We possess enough evidence to say once more that we can be certain that the *Testaments*' authors used available traditions to make a particular point about a particular patriarch (in this case Judah's heroism), but we lack the little bit extra that permits certainty on the nature of the relationships among the witnesses.

The least useful texts proposed as 'source material' are a handful of Qumran fragments Milik associated with the testaments of Judah and Joseph. Milik dubbed 4Q538, two fragments of a late Hasmonean Aramaic work, 'Testament of Judah' (1978: 97-98), saying that the scant remains are the narration of Jacob's sons' second trip to Egypt and Joseph (cf. Gen. 44.1–45.10; *Jub.* 43.1-13). Although *T. Jud.* 12.11-12 only sum–marizes this trip, the existence at Qumran of a precursor to the *Testament of Judah* in 4Q538 is confirmed for Milik by the parallel he discerns between 3Q7 6, 5 + 3, a Herodian text which he deems to be another copy of the work attested in 4Q538, and *T. Jud.* 25.1-2. Milik also identi-fied 4Q539, a late Hasmonean Aramaic manuscript, as the 'Testament of Joseph' (1978: 101-102). While he intimates that isolated references to 'children' and 'loved ones' in frg. 2.2 provide the formal characteristics of a testament, the two phrases hardly suffice as convincing evidence of the narrative framework expected of a testament. However, Milik argues that the remaining content matches elements of *T. Jos.* 14.4-5 (frg. 1) and 15.1–17.2 (frg. 2). On that basis he names the work a 'Testament of Joseph'. But like 4Q215 and 4Q538 the meagre parallels in content do not overcome the absence of the narrative framework distinctive of testaments. Anyway, so little of the Qumran manuscript survives that one can hardly form a reliable judgment about its character. At best we can only say that here again we have little more than textual material that reflects traditions probably known to the authors of the *Testaments*. We certainly do not have anything approaching evidence for pre-Christian testaments of Judah and Joseph.

The materials from Qumran, the Cairo Geniza, and the Mt Athos manuscript of the *Testaments* that parallel parts of *Testament of Levi* present a very different situation. At Qumran a single manuscript from Cave 1 (1Q21; DJD 1: 87-91) and six from Cave 4 (4Q213–214b; DJD 22: 1-71) give Aramaic text that parallels parts of *T. Levi* 8–9; 11–14. These manuscripts also provide new material concerning Levi. From the Cairo Geniza two large fragments of a single manuscript preserve Aramaic parallels for *T. Levi* 6–7; 8–9; 11–13 (Charles and Cowley 1907; Pass and Arendzen 1900). And part of the Cairo Geniza manuscript giving Isaac's priestly instructions to Levi and Levi's life history matches a long addition to the Greek *Testament of Levi* in the Mt Athos manuscript of the *Testaments* at *T. Levi* 18.2 (Charles 1908a [see also additions to the Mt Athos manuscript at *T. Levi* 2.3 and 5.2; the former is paralleled by 4Q213a 1-2; DJD 22: 27-33]). Many have assumed that since much of this fragmentary and disparate material parallels the existing Greek testament, the work may best be reconstructed on the model of the Greek work. They also argue that the existence of such a text proves that the *Testaments*' authors used a pre-existing Jewish work to compose the Greek *Testament of Levi*, which, after all, is strikingly different from the other testaments (de Jonge 1988). Greenfield and Stone first questioned the practice of determining the shape of the Aramaic work on the basis of the Greek testament (Greenfield and Stone 1979). Then I proposed a different reconstruction of the Aramaic text based chiefly on the surviving evidence for that work (Kugler 1996a). What emerges is a document that is very different from the Greek testament. It begins by retelling Gen. 34, and continues with Levi's prayer, a single vision in which Levi is elevated to the priestly office by heavenly angels, Levi's encounter with his father and grandfather in which he is ordained and instructed in the ways of the priesthood, his life history, and his speech on wisdom and his descendants' future (for a comparison of this reconstructed form of *Aramaic Levi* with the *Testament of Levi*, see Chapter 2 and Kugler 1996a: 174-77). In spite of the claim I made in the same 1996 study that comparison of this version of *Aramaic Levi* with the Greek testament permits one to imagine the pre-Christian form of Levi's deathbed address, an 'Original *Testament of Levi*' (Kugler 1996a: 171-220), I now agree with de Jonge that the evidence only confirms that the authors of the Christian testament used some form of a Jewish source text, evidence for which can be found in the diverse witnesses to *Aramaic Levi* (de Jonge 1999; however, I stand by my reconstruction of *Aramaic Levi*). For more on the sources used in *Testament of Levi* and critical discussion of them, see Chapter 2 below.

Provenance, Date, Compositional History and Purpose

Evidence for the *Testaments'* contents, genre, themes, central characters, relationship to other Jewish and Christian works, textual history and source documents have all featured in efforts to sort out the related puzzles of their provenance, date, compositional history and aim. Nevertheless, answers to these questions elude researchers, so that the effort to reach common conclusions on these matters reminds one of the mountain in Phaedrus, *Fables* IV.24 (Perry). It laboured so loudly that in all the region there was great expectation; but like the mouse that the mountain brought forth, the consensus achieved on these issues has been far less significant than had been hoped (for an account of this history, see Slingerland 1977 and Ulrichsen 1991: 15-20; and for the earlier period, see H.J. de Jonge 1975b).

There are three general approaches to the related questions of the *Testaments'* provenance, date, compositional history and purpose (for this schema, see Collins 1984: 342). The dominant view is that Jews first wrote the *Testaments*, and only later were they redacted to serve the interests of the early Christian movement. Already in 1698 J.E. Grabe articulated this basic notion (Grabe 1698). Then in 1884 F. Schnapp treated the *Testaments* to a careful literary-critical analysis. Schnapp posited a compositional history that included an original parenetic Jewish composition, a Jewish redaction that introduced apocalyptic materials, and a final Christian redaction that added yet more eschatological content to the existing Jewish apocalyptic material.

R.H. Charles (1908a, 1908b, 1913), J. Becker (1970, 1974), A. Hultgård (1977, 1980, 1982), and J.H. Ulrichsen (1991) have all sought to elaborate Schnapp's hypothesis of a Jewish precursor to the Christian *Testaments* (also see the work of E. Bickerman 1950; F.-C. Braun 1960; R. Eppel 1930; J. Jervell 1969 [although Jervell concentrates on the Christian form of the *Testaments*, he makes decisions about what is 'interpolated' to do so, and thus belongs to this category of critics]; H.C. Kee 1978, 1983; P. Macky 1969; K.H. Rengstorf 1974; J. Thomas 1969; for summaries and criticisms of the views of these scholars, see M. de Jonge 1960, 1962, 1975b). Relying on literary- and text-critical judgments that ostensibly permitted him to isolate a pre-Christian form of the *Testaments*, Charles concluded that the original *Testaments* came into existence some-time during the reign of John Hyrcanus. They were meant to express Pharisaic support for the Hasmoneans (thus the pro-Levi material). Around the middle of the first century BCE the same Pharisaic group redacted the *Testaments* because of their dissatisfaction with the Hasmo-neans (thus the anti-Levi materials). Finally Christian additions were made after the turn of the era (Charles 1908b). The results of Charles' treatment make themselves abundantly clear in the way he bracketed 'Christian' material in his presentation of the text, and in the extensive notes (especially in 1908b) he devoted to passages which he thought provided evidence of the Jewish stages in the *Testaments*' development.

Even though Charles' views rested in large part on text-critical judg-ments that were almost immediately discredited (Hunkin 1914; Messel 1918) and had long since been deemed untenable (de Jonge 1953; Stone 1969), J. Becker (1970) persisted in accepting the value of the Armenian text as a pointer to a pre-Christian form of the work. Becker concluded that a Hellenistic-Jewish author created the *Testaments* perhaps as early as the late third century BCE as an exercise in moral exhortation. Later the *Testaments* were redacted in Hellenistic-Jewish circles to include more synagogue homiletical material, the L.J. and S.E.R. passages, and still other apocalyptic and messianic passages. Only later were the Christian additions made. The results of Becker's text- and literary-critical efforts populate the pages of his dense 1970 monograph, as well as his 1974 commentary on the *Testaments*.

In 1969 Jacob Jervell and Johannes Thomas (together with Burchard on the Armenian text; see above) published their views on the *Testaments*' origin, compositional history and purpose. Assuming a Jewish original, Jervell tried to ascertain the nature of the Christian redactor of the *Testaments*. Jervell concluded that the redactor was uninterested in the ethical material, and focused almost exclusively on the predictive pas-sages. Citing the universalism of the *Testaments*, Jervell suggested that the redactor changed the prophecy of the Jewish original to show that Gentiles are saved, Jews opposed Jesus, and that Jesus would return as a law-renewing messiah to provide Jews another chance for salvation. Thus the Christian redaction was made to express concern for Israel's fate. Principally because of its 'Jewish-Christian' Christology, Jervell dates the *Testaments* to around 100 CE.

Thomas (1969) provides a still more definite portrait of the *Testaments*' development, date and purpose. His interest, the *Sitz im Leben* of the

Testaments, compels him to address the history of the text. Thomas insists, against Charles, that the anti-Levi material was original, and that members of the Qumran community or parties to the conflict over the high priesthood in the second century BCE added the pro-Levi passages. The anti-Levi material he believed to be from the days of Jason and Menelaus. The emphasis on Joseph suggests to Thomas that the *Testaments* were aimed at Jews in Egypt. Overall, he describes the work as a *Diasporasendschreiben* to Egyptian Jews that encouraged them to be like their hero, Joseph.

In two volumes published in 1977 and 1982, A. Hultgård carried on the tradition of asserting there to have been a pre-Christian, Jewish *Testaments* (see also Hultgård 1980). Hultgård focused on the eschatological passages in the *Testaments,* and his approach to the task of isolating this pre-Christian form of the *Testaments* is eclectic. Although not explicitly literary-critical, his work relies in part on observing in the *Testaments* seams, inconsistencies and the like. At the same time he thinks that past scholarship has made too much of such literary characteristics and has ignored the possibility that those rough edges are simply the result of the authors' use of divergent traditional materials. Hultgård also relies on text-critical judgments (see especially his 1982 volume). Against all the evidence to the contrary, he thinks that the Armenian text can assist one in ascertaining pre-Christian forms of the individual *Testaments*. In his 1977 book Hultgård asserts that the compositional history began with the composition of a Levi-apocryphon, evidence for which is available in the Levi materials discussed above. He describes this as a 'Zadokite' document related to, but not from, the Essenes and the Dead Sea Scrolls. The Levi-apocryphon expresses the view of a Jerusalem levitical-priestly group that goes back as far as the third century BCE. The apocryphon underwent an indiscernible redactional history within this 'levitical' group through to the first century BCE. Around the turn of the era a separate Jewish group took up the developed apocryphon and expanded it, making its views more universalistic, especially by adding the ideal saviour passages (in particular *T. Levi* 18; *T. Jud.* 24). Lastly, Christians redacted the *Testaments* for their own use in the second century CE.

The most recent large-scale study of the *Testaments* that follows the Schnapp–Charles approach comes from J.H. Ulrichsen (1991). Like his predecessors, Ulrichsen accepts the basic notion that there must have been a Jewish form of the *Testaments*, but also like his predecessors he feels compelled to create yet another new hypothesis regarding the shape of that work. Thus his book, although interesting, only further clouds an already obscure horizon. Ulrichsen adopts and reworks Schnapp's basic thesis. Using a mostly literary-critical approach, he posits a five-stage compositional history for the *Testaments*. The *Grundschrift* was a Jewish parenetical work that used Joseph as an ideal figure. It was composed in Hebrew or Aramaic around 200 BCE in Palestine. Jewish redactors added most of the prophetic and eschatological-apocalyptic material between 160 and 100/63 BCE. In a third stage before the turn of the era more Hebrew or Aramaic material of varied character was added. In the fourth stage, which Ulrichsen dates to the first century CE, still more assorted material was added and the *Testaments* were translated into Greek. The fifth stage is marked by the addition of Christian elements, probably beginning in the second century CE.

A second approach to the questions of provenance, date, compositional history and purpose also assigns the *Testaments* to Jewish circles. This position differs from the first, however, in the insistence that the *Testaments'* supposedly Christian passages actually derive from the Jewish authors and keepers of the Dead Sea Scrolls, the Essenes.

A. Dupont-Sommer (1953) first associated the *Testaments* with Qumran and the Dead Sea Scrolls in a systematic manner (but compare Audet 1952, 1953; Kuhn 1952; Rabin 1952). Dupont-Sommer's position was quite simple: the *Testaments* were composed entirely at Qumran by the Essenes, and the elevated priest in the *Testament of Levi* was the community's Teacher of Righteousness while the wicked priests of chapters 10, 14, 15, and 16 were those who persecuted this righteous figure. Thus Dupont-Sommer takes the view that the *Testaments* were 'neither Christian nor interpolated' (Slingerland 1977: 46). Benedikt Otzen (1953) countered Dupont-Sommer's confident linkage of the scrolls with the *Testaments*. He confirmed thematic connections between the two bodies of literature (ethics, theology, demons and angels, and notions of the messiah), but effectively discounted the historical connections Dupont-Sommer made between figures in the *Testaments* and in the scrolls. Nevertheless, M. Philonenko (1960) repeated and developed Dupont-Sommer's claim that the messianic passages usually construed as Christian are in fact Essene. However, he also determined that the original *Testaments* were composed in (undefined) Jewish circles, and only later were interpolated by the Qumran community. Thus for him, too, the messianic references are not to Jesus, but to the Teacher of Righteousness. And like Dupont-Sommer, Philonenko thinks that the *Testaments* help one to reconstruct the history of the Qumran community.

Like the theories regarding a general Jewish origin of the *Testaments*, the range of opinion expressed within the parameters of the Qumran-origins hypothesis undermines confidence in its explanatory power. Moreover, the notion that the *Testaments* were composed among the

Essenes at Qumran and that the messianic passages refer to the Teacher of Righteousness seem utterly implausible to most readers. For instance, Philonenko's reading of the *Testaments'* messianic passages too often ignore more obvious and apt parallels with New Testament references to Jesus (compare, for example, *T. Gad* 2.3-5 and Mt. 27.3-9; de Jonge 1960 offers a discussion of this and other passages addressed by Philonenko). Finally, broader publication of the scrolls has demonstrated their authors and keepers to have been particularly fascinated with the details of the law, an interest that lacks prominence in the *Testaments* (*pace* Slingerland 1986).

The work of Marinus de Jonge exemplifies a third approach to the *Testaments* and the question of their provenance, date, compositional history and purpose. To recall the orphaned-child metaphor I used at the beginning of this chapter, de Jonge solves the problem of the *Testaments'* uncertain origins by saying that the parents of the child often thought to have been its adoptive guardians, Christians, were in fact their 'biological' progenitors all along (for a treatment of earlier proponents of this view, see Slingerland 1977: 6-15). Because this splendidly simple solution to the problem has the extraordinary merit of having been worked out over the course of nearly a half-century, it deserves close attention.

In 1953 de Jonge resurrected the pre-Schnapp hypothesis that the *Testaments*, though perhaps incorporating considerable Jewish source material, were essentially Christian compositions. After demonstrating the implausibility of the Conybeare–Charles method of using the Armenian text to reconstruct a pre-Christian *Testaments*, de Jonge showed that the Christian materials cannot be disentangled from the *Testaments* by means of text-critical analysis. Then through a source-critical examination of the semitic parallel materials for the *Testament of Levi*, *Testament of Naphtali* and *Testament of Judah*, de Jonge showed that in all cases the sources or related materials had been adapted to reflect Christian interests. Similarly the parallel between *Jub.* 33.9-20 and *T. Reub.* 3.9–4.5 supported the same conclusion. To seal his source-critical argument that a Christian redactor-composer was responsible for the overall composition of the *Testaments*, de Jonge turned to the *Testament of Issachar*. Although it relies solely on the Septuagint of Genesis for its non-Masoretic parallel material, it still conforms to the style and pattern of the testaments that used semitic source material. De Jonge also demonstrated at the thematic level the thoroughly Christian character of the work. He noted how the S.E.R. and L.J. passages were, though in all likelihood borrowed patterns, adapted completely to the Christian aim of the *Testaments*. Thus the 'sin' and 'return' parts of the pattern often relate to Jesus, and the Levi-Judah pattern was made to refer to Jesus as well. He also noted that the similar introduction and conclusion shared by each of the *Testaments* provides further evidence of a common (Christian) authorship. In the light of these and other observations, de Jonge posited a date of 190 to 225 CE for the *Testaments* and assigned their composition to an 'ordinary Christian' because of their lack of concern for the higher christological debates of the era. He also assigned the *Testaments* a non-Palestinian provenance because of their poor sense of the region's geography.

Over the course of nearly half a century, de Jonge has modified some of his stronger statements regarding the exclusively Christian character of the *Testaments*, but he has also advanced other aspects of his thesis. Especially in light of the evidence of the Scrolls (see, for example, Milik 1955) de Jonge quickly—and correctly—accepted the notion that, although the *Testaments* are in their present form a Christian work, they probably underwent a long compositional and redactional history that included a lengthy period during which they may have developed in Jewish circles (de Jonge 1960, 1962). He also widened and lowered his estimate of the period in which the Christian form of the *Testaments* took shape, suggesting that it may have come about sometime late in the second century CE.

Nevertheless, de Jonge has never withdrawn his assertion that there is no getting behind the text of the *Testaments* to some pre-Christian, Jewish *Vorlage*. He remains firm in his view that literary criticism is too subjective an exercise to be of much use in establishing a pre-Christian form, and that traditio-historical criticism only produces useless speculation. Likewise, he still rejects text criticism's capacity to provide us with anything more ancient than a ninth-century Christian text. Consequently he steadfastly insists that the best place to begin one's study of the *Testaments* is with the Christian work that remains to us. It is the meaning of that work that we must investigate.

De Jonge has made significant headway toward the goal of understanding the *Testaments* as a Christian composition. In addition to the commentary on the *Testaments* he co-wrote with H.W. Hollander (1985) and his contributions to *ANRW* (1987) and *ABD* (1992) he has addressed separately a number of substantive issues related to the *Testaments*. He has demonstrated that the *Testaments'* parenesis simultaneously reflects Hellenistic, Hellenistic-Jewish and Christian ethics, and therefore cannot be relied upon as a resource in establishing a Jewish origin for the *Testaments* (de Jonge 1989a, 1990). He has directed attention to early Christian authors who also understand the pre-Mosaic ancestors as the mouthpiece for God's eternal law, obedience to which has salvific power (de Jonge 1985a, 1985b, 1993). He has also devoted attention to the nettlesome diversity of the future-oriented passages (de Jonge 1986a, 1986b), suggesting that while the conflicts among them probably result from the diverse sources used by the authors of the *Testaments*, and from post-second-century Christian redactional activity, consistent patterns can be found among them. For example, passages on the salvation of the ancestors and the Gentiles indicate that anyone who keeps God's universal law and/or believes in Jesus as messiah will be resurrected in the end of days. In fact, many of the S.E.R. and ideal saviour passages prove that God will offer salvation through Jesus even to those descendants of the patriarchs who have rebelled against the law, and against the sons of Levi and Judah. As for this universal, heavenly redeemer, his advent is announced in all of the L.J. passages that connect God's plan of salvation with an individual from the tribes of Levi and Judah. Most of all, de Jonge has also drawn attention to the fact that the future-oriented passages are chiefly concerned with the fate of Israel (de Jonge 1986a).

Drawing from the particulars of the foregoing observations, de Jonge has made some general claims regarding the overall aim of the *Testaments* as a Christian work. They are, in large part, parenetical Christian compositions dedicated to instructing Christians in proper conduct and to enlisting the instruction of the Old Testament patriarchs in that enterprise. He adds, though, that the *Testaments* are also concerned with the salvation of Israel. To quote de Jonge himself, '[t]hose responsible for the "Christian Testaments" were firmly convinced that they were transmitting, i.q. bringing out more clearly, what the sons of Jacob had meant to say all the time' (de Jonge 1985c: 274), and the content of that message was that keeping God's universal law, which was reaffirmed by Jesus, leads to salvation. As such this composition should be understood, 'if not as a missionary tractate, at least as having informed Christians in their contacts with Jews' (de Jonge 1986a: 211). Thus the '*Testaments* as a whole have to be approached as a witness to the continuity in thought and ideas between Judaism (in particular Hellenistic Judaism) and early Christianity' (1989b: 206).

It should already be clear that I find de Jonge's approach to the questions of the *Testaments*' provenance, date, compositional history and purpose to be the most judicious of those surveyed here. (In this I would include his judgment that we cannot know in which Christian community of the second century CE the *Testaments* were completed, apart from the fact that Palestine does not seem to be a good candidate. The work's poor sense of Palestinian geography speaks in favour of that view [de Jonge 1953; Hollander and de Jonge 1985: 85], as does its lack of concern for cultic law, something to which an author appealing to Palestinian or Jerusalem Jews surely would have devoted some attention.

Not even the *Testaments'* reliance on traditions otherwise preserved in Aramaic [*Testament of Levi*] and Hebrew [*Testament of Naphtali* and *Testament of Judah*] helps here, inasmuch as those traditions clearly travelled throughout the Mediterranean region [fragments of *Aramaic Levi* turn up in the Cairo Geniza as well as at Qumran; note also that a Greek translation of parts of *Aramaic Levi* appear at Mt Athos].) While converts to de Jonge's view are remarkably slow in coming, his insistence that we cannot achieve sufficient consensus on a pre-Christian form of the *Testaments* to make the pursuit of one worthwhile seems destined to win the day. The vast and seemingly irreconcilable differences among the proposals made by critics like Ulrichsen, Becker, Jervell, Thomas, Hultgård, Charles, Dupont-Sommer and Philonenko would seem to assure this outcome. My own experience with developing theories regarding the transitional stages between a work like *Aramaic Levi* and the *Testaments* also reveals the difficulty of achieving sufficient agreement to make the undertaking particularly valuable. Thus de Jonge's concomitant commitment to ascertaining a sense of the meaning of the Christian *Testaments* is especially to be embraced.

Our Approach to the Testaments

For many, de Jonge's focus on the Christian *Testaments* has effectively settled the questions of the work's parentage, intended audience and general purpose. But somewhat neglected are the landmarks he and others have uncovered that point the way to understanding how the *Testaments* may have also been received by Jews. From his observations—and ours regarding the *Testaments'* contents, genre, themes, main figures, and relationships with other works and sources—one may conclude that in addition to addressing Christian believers, the *Testaments'* rhetoric could easily have testified to Jews as well. And their testimony would have been that Israel's most ancient ancestors promulgated all the law that was necessary for a faithful life in God's sight. Moreover, the life and message of the Christian deliverer Jesus was entirely coherent with the ancestors' proclamation *and* with the standards of conduct set by popular Graeco-Roman philosophy; and anyway, belief in the saviour by itself earned salvation. Therefore, the *Testaments* urged Jews to accept Jesus and his teaching as their redemption. To return again to the child–parent metaphor, it seems that the *Testaments* could have been read in antiquity as having emerged from the womb of a Christian community not only to instruct their immediate family about God's age-old moral norms, but also to appeal to their mother's sister, the people of Israel, regarding God's wishes for them.

The remainder of the Guide focuses on explicating the ways in which the *Testaments* might have achieved these effects in Jewish and Christian audiences. Chapter 2 examines the testaments individually, focusing on their relationships to the biblical record about the patriarchs, their special characteristics and critical problems, and their contributions to the *Testaments'* likely effect, and especially to persuading Jews to the Christian cause. Chapter 3 explores some of the more subtle ways in which the *Testaments* use the Jewish and Christian scriptures of the Graeco-Roman era—the 'Old Testament' in Greek translation—to draw their audience ever deeper into their argument about God's intentions for all God's people.

Further Reading

Throughout this chapter and Chapters 2 and 3 I cite the works of Philo and Josephus and various Graeco-Roman authors. After the citations the reader will notice a name in parentheses or brackets; it is the editor of an English translation of the text in question. The translations, usually to be found in the Loeb Classical Library, are included in the General Bibliography under the editor's name.

E. Ferguson (1993) provides convenient introductions to Philo, Josephus and most of the Graeco-Roman authors cited here.

Text
The critical edition of the *Testaments* is from de Jonge *et al.* (1978). The complex issue of the work's textual history is most easily accessed in English in de Jonge (1987).

English translations can be found in Kee (1978), Hollander and de Jonge (1985), and Sparks (1984) (note that the translation in Sparks was provided by de Jonge). The translation in Hollander and de Jonge is to be preferred over all others, and is the one used here, unless indicated otherwise.

Genre
On the question of the *Testaments'* genre, Kolenkow (1975) and Collins (1984) are most especially to be consulted (see also Winter 1994). In addition, von Nordheim (1980) is a significant voice on the question of the work's genre as a whole. For the genres within the *Testaments*, see also Aschermann (1955), mindful, however, of the critique offered by H.W. Hollander (1981: 11-12).

Treatments of Main Themes and Figures

Much attention has been given to the *Testament of Levi*, but little to the figure of Levi in the *Testaments*. To his credit, de Jonge (1999) has moved to remedy that lacuna, but more needs to be done of the same judicious character. Others attending to Levi as a key figure include Hultgård (1977, 1980); Kugel (1993); and to a lesser extent, Stone (1988b). See also VanderKam (1999), although his study is directed mostly at the vexing question of the literary relationships among the *Testament of Levi*, *Jubilees* 31, and the Aramaic predecessor document to the *Testament of Levi*.

Oddly, little work has been devoted to the role of Judah in the *Testaments*. Many of the treatments of messianism in the *Testaments*, of course, are inevitably interested in Judah (see, for example, Beasley-Murray 1947; Collins 1995). One should also consult Wassén (1994).

Joseph has been thoroughly researched as a key figure in the *Testaments*. Here one must consult most especially H.W. Hollander (1981). But see also Niehoff (1992).

De Jonge has treated the main themes of the *Testaments* (see the list of his publications in the bibliography). One can also consult Kee (1978) for the ethical dimensions of the *Testaments* and Macky (1969) for theology, theodicy and eschatology.

Source Documents

De Jonge (1987) provides the most straightforward entry into this complex set of issues. Of course, one should also consult the primary texts as they are discussed above. See on the Levi material especially the array of articles from de Jonge; Kugler (1996a, 1996b); VanderKam (1999).

Provenance, Date, Compositional History and Purpose

Treatments of these topics, as the discussion above points out, are legion so long as the concern is with a pre-Christian composition. For summaries see M. de Jonge (1975b), Slingerland (1977) and Ulrichsen (1991: 15-20); and for the earlier period, see H.J. de Jonge (1975b).

Only de Jonge has interested himself consistently with these questions as they relate to the Christian form of the work. For his arguments, see his works listed in the bibliography, especially those dating after 1985.

2

A CLOSER LOOK AT THE TESTAMENTS OF THE TWELVE PATRIARCHS: SPECIAL CHARACTERISTICS, CRITICAL POINTS OF INTEREST AND MEANING

Now we turn our attention to the individual testaments. This chapter introduces the reader to each testament's contents, peculiar characteristics and points of critical interest. The explicit use of Scripture throughout the *Testaments* receives special emphasis. These specific objectives serve the larger goal of demonstrating each speech's contribution to the work's likely effect on Christian *and* Jewish recipients.

Testament of Reuben

This testament takes as its point of departure Reuben's sexual indiscretion with Bilhah, his father's concubine (Gen. 35.22; 49.4). That biographical datum forms the nucleus around which almost everything else is gathered. Thus Reuben's alternating biographical reflections and moral exhortations against impurity take root in his experience with Bilhah, as does his implicit definition of 'impurity', πορνεία, as sexual impropriety (*T. Reub.* 1.6–6.4). Only the eschatological material, a 'double L. passage' (Hollander and de Jonge 1985: 105) stands apart from the Bilhah episode (*T. Reub.* 6.5-12). The testament serves well as a subtle introduction to the *Testaments'* argument regarding God's intentions toward Israel.

The theme of this testament—sexual restraint and indiscretion—reappears in others (Judah; Issachar; Joseph). It also calls attention to the fact that the authors of the *Testaments* embraced a common Jewish, Christian and Hellenistic sexual ethic. That ethic called for sexual restraint, especially inside of marriage, and promoted intercourse largely for purposes of procreation (see the full discussion of the ethic as it appears in the *Testaments* and in Jewish, Christian and Hellenistic texts in de Jonge 1990). In Reuben's case restraint was lacking, and πορνεία controlled his actions.

Testament of Reuben 2.3–3.8, a double exposition of the seven (in fact they work out to be eight) spirits that animate human action, interrupts the otherwise consistent pattern of exhortation followed by illustrative biographical material in 1.6–6.4. Although some deem this a late interpolation (Ulrichsen 1991: 71-78), the evidence indicates that the authors of the testament included it. *T. Reub.* 1.6 anticipates 2.3–3.8, and 3.9-10 is a well-integrated resumptive introduction (de Jonge 1953: 75-77). Of course, this conclusion hardly requires that the authors of the testament composed the passage; they could just as easily have adapted a source available to them. Indeed, the seven spirits of 2.3–3.2 reflect the Stoic notions of the parts of the soul (Aetius 4.21.1-4 [Long and Sedley 1987: 315-16] Philo, *Quaest. in Gen.* 1.75 [Colson *et al.*]; Kee 1978: 266). And although some of the 'spirits' mentioned in 3.3-8 resemble interests expressed throughout the *Testaments* (fornication for Reuben; fighting for Judah), the correspondences are incomplete, indicating that this list was also a source adapted to its context. In any case, the lists function clearly enough when Reuben explains the effect of the spirits: 'And so every young man perishes, darkening his mind from the truth and not under-standing the law of God nor obeying the admonitions of his fathers, as I also suffered in my youth' (3.8; note the equation of truth, law and the instruction of the fathers). The vices, it seems, undermine truth, the keeping of the law, and adherence to the fathers' instructions.

Another notable item in the biography-parenesis is the parallel between much of the biographical material in the testament and parts of *Jubilees*. These further indicate the author's compilatory impulse in telling Reuben's story. They also suggest something of the authors' exegetical sophistication. James Kugel (1995) notes the shared motif of Reuben's sighting of Bilhah bathing naked in *Jub.* 33.2 and *T. Reub.* 3.11 (the water of her bath, says Kugel, is based on the reference to Reuben as 'unstable as water' in Gen. 49.4). He also notes that *Jubilees* and the testament explain the juxtaposition of 'And Israel heard of it' with 'the sons of Jacob were twelve' in Gen. 35.22 as the result of Jacob's rejection of Bilhah after he discovered the indiscretion (*Jub.* 33.9 and *T. Reub.* 3.15; because of the cessation of intercourse there were no more than twelve sons).

The use of συνείδησις, 'conscience', in *T. Reub.* 4.3 also draws attention to the combined biography-parenesis. Reuben says that his 'conscience' oppresses him on account of his sin. Depending on the date assigned to the *Testaments* and their origin among Jews or Christians, some suggest that this could be the first known use of the term in a Jewish text. However, without a consensus on the date and origin of a pre-Christian form of the *Testaments* it is impossible to make much of this possibility (although the use of the same term with much the same meaning in Rom. 2.15 does gives one pause). Anyway, of much greater interest here is the fact that συνείδησις is typical of Stoic thought (Kee 1978), and therefore reflects in its appearance in 4.3 the *Testaments'* habit of linking pious behaviour to common Graeco-Roman standards of conduct.

Although a relatively small matter, the shared use of the command to 'flee impurity' in *T. Reub.* 5.5 and 1 Cor. 6.18a has also attracted attention because of its implications for the relationship between the *Testaments* and the New Testament. Brian Rosner examines the relationship between the two passages and concludes either that both Paul and the *Testaments'* authors could have relied independently on a shared interpretative tradition related to Gen. 39 (the apparent biblical basis for the reference), or that Paul was dependent on the *Testament of Reuben* (Rosner 1992). Rosner prefers the latter option, but de Jonge questions Rosner's certainty on the matter, suggesting that the directions in which the connections run in this case, and throughout the *Testaments*, are not so clear (de Jonge 1995: 107; there are also looser connections between *T. Reub.* 3.5 and 2 Pet. 2.3; *T. Reub.* 5.5 and 2 Pet. 2.4, cited by Charles 1908b: 7, 12).

One cannot fail to notice as well the first Joseph-as-model passage to appear in the *Testaments*. In 4.8-10 Joseph's sexual restraint vis-à-vis the Egyptian woman contrasts with Reuben's lustful nature. Notably the reference in 4.9 to magicians and love potions parallels the extrabiblical tradition repeated in *T. Jos.* 6.

The reference to the Watchers in 5.6-7 is unusual, but easily explained, given the authors' aims (cf. *T. Naph.* 3.5; Gen. 6.1-4). Because of the authors' focus on the problems women present for men (see a fuller discussion of this theme in the *Testaments* in the section on the *Testament of Judah* below), here the women are made to play the role of the sexual aggressors, not the Watchers.

The unusually complex, yet truncated L.J. passage in *T. Reub.* 6.5-12 provides a final special characteristic of this testament. Though it appears to be an L.J. passage, it only anticipates the sovereignty of Levi (6.7; Judah [and Reuben, Dan and Joseph; cf. Num. 2.10, 18, 25] are mentioned only as an aside) and the unsuccessful rebellion of Reuben's descendants against Levi's kingship (6.5-6). Before and after a general exhortation that seems somewhat out of place (6.9), Reuben urges his children to obey Levi because his legal teaching is authentic and he controls the sacrificial system until the coming of an 'anointed high priest' (6.8), and because God has chosen Levi to be king over all nations forever and to die for Israel in 'visible and invisible wars' (6.10-12). The closing reference to the death of the descendant of Levi ties the passage loosely to Jesus (e.g., Rom. 5.6-8; 14.15; 2 Cor. 5.15).

Within the prediction passage Reuben makes a single, oblique reference to the double commandment that dominates the exhortations in the
Testaments. In 6.8 he urges his sons to proper piety *in relationship to God* by
telling them to obey Levi's leadership in sacrifice. In 6.9 he then commands them to 'do truth, each one to his neighbour and to bear love each
one for his brother'.

The *Testament of Reuben* fits well within the general understanding of
the *Testaments* developed at the end of the Guide's first chapter. Although
it is Reuben's first-born status that assures this speech's place at the
beginning of the *Testaments*, his testament functions effectively as the
opening address among the twelve. The introduction and conclusion
include all of the elements that will be encountered throughout the
Testaments (and more; see the presence of some of Reuben's brothers at
his speech in 1.4-5). Seesawing back and forth between biography and
parenesis clearly establishes the ties between those two parts of the
Testaments. The inclusion of the Stoic lists in 2.3–3.8 and the use of the
word συνείδησις in 4.3 signal the identification of Graeco-Roman philosophy with the teaching of the patriarchs. Likewise, the echoes of Prov.
6.24-25 LXX in 3.10; 4.1, 8 indicate the *Testaments*' reliance on the Septuagint, and the repetition of traditions preserved in *Jubilees* shows the
authors' familiarity with the wider Jewish literature of the era. The brief
future-oriented passage (6.5-12) announces most of the themes to come:
it predicts the rebellion of Reuben's descendants against Levi (and Judah)
and implies their rejection of Jesus as well (6.5-8), but it also looks forward to the redemption of even the most rebellious through the agency
of the messiah to come (v. 12). And the future prediction introduces,
albeit allusively, the *Testaments*' obsession with the fulfilment of God's
double commandment. Though equally indirect, the connection between
Jesus and the tribe of Levi turns up here for the first time.

Testament of Simeon

The *Testament of Simeon* dwells on Simeon's jealousy that prompted him
to hate Joseph so much as to wish to kill him (and Judah too for upsetting
his homicidal plans; Gen. 37.26-28). Simeon tells his children of his envy
and its consequences and exhorts them to avoid the same mistake (2.2–
5.1). He also warns them against impurity (5.2-3) and states that he had
learnt from the writings of Enoch that impurity would lead to the
destruction of them and their descendants (5.4-6). But the testament also
features an alternative future, one that includes Simeon's own
resurrection if his children and their descendants take his warning to
heart (6.1–7.3). The unusually full conclusion mentions the synchrony of

a war with the Egyptians and the transfer of Simeon's bones to Hebron (8.2; cf. *Jub.* 46.9-10), the protection of Joseph's bones in Egypt to prevent the gloom that would descend upon the land for lack of his beneficent presence (8.3-4), and the residence of Simeon's descendants in Egypt until the exodus (9.1). In particular, this testament strengthens the ties between Graeco-Roman ethical standards and the teaching of the patriarchs and it provides the first unmistakable allusion to Jesus as a saviour descended from the tribes of Levi and Judah.

The testament's inconsistent use of the terms ζῆλος ('jealousy') and φθόνος ('envy') to describe Simeon's vice has long drawn interest. The work is entitled ΠΕΡΙ ΦΘΟΝΟΥ in most manuscripts (de Jonge *et al.* 1978: 14), yet φθόνος first occurs at 2.13. Before that ζῆλος appears twice (2.6, 7), and again in 4.5, 9 (but in v. 5 with φθόνος; cf. *T. Gad* 7.2, 4; *T. Benj.* 4.4). Otherwise φθόνος occurs alone in the rest of the testament (2.14; 3.1, 2, 3, 4, 6; 4.7; 6.2). φθόνος has a negative sense in some of the other testaments (*T. Gad* 3.3; 4.5; 7.2; *T. Dan* 2.5; *T. Jos.* 1.3; *T. Benj.* 4.4; 7.5; 8.1), while, *T. Levi* 6.3; *T. Ash.* 4.5 use ζῆλος positively to describe zeal for God and purity. One could solve the conundrum by reading *T. Sim.* 4.7 as the heading of a section dealing with φθόνος, and treating ζῆλος in 4.9 as an expression of its subsidiary character to φθόνος. However that is not an easy case to make. Becker's solution—assigning the parenesis regarding jealousy and envy to a later redactor—is no more successful (Becker 1970: 326-35). Hollander and de Jonge are probably correct in their judgment that the testament simply uses the two terms synonymously (cf. the similarly free use of the two as parallel expressions for the emotion that leads to ἀδελφοκτονία in 1 Clement 3–6 [Lake]; Hollander and de Jonge: 1985: 110). The similarly synonymous use of the two terms in *T. Dan* 1.6; 2.5 supports this judgment.

On a related note, the testament's focus on φθόνος further proves the connection between the *Testaments* and Graeco-Roman philosophy. φθόνος is a very popular *topos* in Greek philosophy and classical moral discourse (Plato, *Lysis* 215D; *Philebus* 49D [Bury *et al.*]; Plutarch, *Moralia* 536F [Babbitt *et al.*]). And as the discussion in Chapter 3 below proves, Simeon's account of the topic sounds all the traditional notes.

Much of Simeon's biography (2.6-14) builds on references in Gen. 42.19, 24 to Simeon's incarceration during the brothers' first visit to Egypt to purchase food. The testament reports that Simeon's imprisonment was recompense for his fratricidal envy for Joseph. This claim and Simeon's braggadocio about his valour and strength (2.3-5), surely grow from his biblical reputation for violence (Gen. 34.25; 49.5-7). Both themes may also be related to an extrabiblical tradition that Simeon and Levi harboured particular animosity toward Joseph (*T. Ps.-J.* Gen. 37.19

[Maher]; *Targ. Neof.* Gen. 49 [McNamara]; Ginzberg 1909–38: V, 328, 348 provides further citations and the suggestion that Gad replaces Levi in the *Testaments* [cf. *T. Zeb.* 2.1; 3.2; 4.2] to spare Levi's reputation).

Several other items in the biography require attention as well. In 2.7-8 we hear for the first time of opposing spirits or angels, one a spirit of jealousy and the other God's angel. This foreshadows the *Testaments'* nearly dualistic angelology that comes to the fore in the *Testament of Asher*. But even here one can see that the *Testaments* stop short of full-blown dualism. After all, Simeon's jealousy is what drives him in the end, not the spirit itself. Also, Joseph serves here not so much as the paradigm of virtue as the victim of vice and the illustration of its ill effects on others. In 2.6 Simeon directs his jealousy at Joseph and in 2.8-9 Simeon's murderous intentions lead to Joseph's sale.

Simeon's parenesis (3.1–5.3) confirms that the angelology is not dual-istic. It takes up the effect of the spirits of envy and deceit (3.1) to make clear the importance of human initiative in relationship to them. *T. Sim.* 3.5 states, 'If a man flees to the Lord the evil spirits run from him'.

Also in the parenesis Simeon introduces a more direct reference to the double commandment than the one in Reuben's speech. He says in 5.2, 'And now my children make your hearts good before the Lord and make your ways straight before men'. The reward is grace before God and humanity.

Simeon's future predictions, attributed to Enoch, begin with an announcement that builds on the curiously-named weapon in Gen. 49.5-7, and it gives bad news to Simeon's descendants. An L. passage, 5.4-6 predicts that Simeon's children will rebel violently with the 'sword' (Gen. 49.5) against Levi, but Levi will prevail, leaving none of Simeon's descendants 'for sovereignty as Jacob prophesied in his blessing' (5.6; cf. Gen. 49.6).

An unusual feature in Simeon's future predictions is his use of a hymn to proclaim the alternative future his tribe could experience if his descendants heed his advice (6.2-7). Probably a source incorporated by the authors, the hymn not only anticipates Simeon's resurrection at the end (6.7; but see also 6.2, and the comments of Hollander and de Jonge 1985: 123), but also the glory of all Simeonites (6.2), the fall of Israel's traditional enemies (6.3-4), the glory of Shem, ancestor of all Israel (6.5a; cf. Gen. 11.10-12), and the redemption of all humanity (in the name of Adam; 6.5c). All of these events coincide with the appearance of God on earth in human form (6.5b).

Testament of Simeon 7.1-2 has played a notable role in the debate over the *Testaments'* messianism. It illustrates the variety of ways scholars have found to interpret the evidence. Over forty years ago A.J.B. Higgins asserted that the passage proves the *Testaments*' anticipation of a Davidic messiah and an associated, non-messianic levitical high priest (1953). Then, when de Jonge's (resurrected) hypothesis of a Christian *Testaments* persuaded Higgins, he reversed his position and agreed that 7.1-2 refers to Jesus alone (1966–67). But most recently Ulrichsen has insisted that 7.2 is a Christian redaction of an originally Jewish text (1991: 83-84)!

Simeon's testament advances the argument of the *Testaments* on several fronts and it introduces for the first time a number of the strategies for making that argument. It extends the treatment of Joseph as the paradigm of morality (4.4, 6) and it introduces him as the victim of his vice-driven brothers (4.2), and as a benefactor of his own goodness (5.1; in *T. Reub.* 4.8 the theme already makes a fleeting appearance). The testament's discussion of the Hellenistic *topos* of envy enlarges the implicit argument that Graeco-Roman standards of conduct are coterminous with the norms proposed by the patriarchs. Simeon's allusion to the double commandment as a key to conquering vice is more explicit than Reuben's reference. And for the first time a patriarch's resurrection is associated with the coming of the saviour (6.2-7) and the saviour's identity as one who comes from the tribes of Levi and Judah is made clear (7.1-2).

Testament of Levi

Levi's valediction, ostensibly about 'the priesthood and arrogance', ἱερωσυνῆς καὶ ὑπερηφάνιας, begins (1.1–2.1) and ends (19.1-5) in much the same way as the other testaments. But the rest of the testament's contents prove that otherwise it departs radically from the standard pattern of biography, parenesis and future prediction. After a brief reference to the violent incident at Shechem (2.2; Gen. 34) Levi expresses his grief at the human condition and prays to God for salvation (2.3-4), has a vision (2.5–6.2), describes more completely his attack on Shechem (6.3–7.4), has another vision (8.1-19), and receives confirmation of the priesthood he received in his visions from his father and priestly instruction from his grandfather (9.1-14). In a first S.E.R. passage Levi foretells his descendants' rebellion against the messiah (10.1-5), then reverts to biography, reciting serially the events of his life (11.1–12.7). Next comes parenesis with Levi exhorting his children to get wisdom and to keep God's law (13.1-9). A double S.E.R. passage foretells (again) his descendants' future iniquity as priests, their rejection of the messiah, and eventual restoration by the messiah (14.1–16.5). And finally, Levi recounts once more the priesthood's decline and its termination and replacement with the messianic high priest (17.1–18.14). This complex valediction, as we will see, epitomizes the *Testaments*' claims regarding God's intentions for Israel.

Levi's speech is peculiar and challenging in many respects. Perhaps most intriguing, but equally vexing, is the possibility of using the source materials introduced in Chapter 1 to trace the testament's compositional history and determine from that history the Jewish origin of the *Testaments* as a whole. The challenge has tempted many, and even though it departs from our focus on the present form of the *Testaments*, the history of those attempts requires attention here.

Since the discovery of the first parallel materials in the Cairo Geniza, scholars have sought to identify further sources for Levi's speech. All agree that several Aramaic manuscripts from Qumran belong to a work, *Aramaic Levi*, which contains passages similar to *T. Levi* 8–9; 11–14 and other material not known before the discovery of the scrolls. (The precise number of Qumran manuscripts of *Aramaic Levi* is debated. Greenfield and Stone, the official editors, counted six manuscripts from Cave 4, four more than Milik determined as the manuscripts' first editor [Milik 1955]; in any case, see now 1Q21; DJD 1: 87-91; 4Q213–214b; DJD 22: 1-71.) Furthermore, the two large fragments of a single Cairo Geniza codex provide an Aramaic text similar to *T. Levi* 6–7; 8–9; 11–13. And a lengthy addition to the Greek Mt Athos manuscript of the *Testaments* at *T. Levi* 18.2 provides material that parallels much of the Aramaic Cairo Geniza manuscript. Milik's and Puech's association of additional Qumran Aramaic manuscripts with *Aramaic Levi* in relation to *T. Levi* 16–18 are to be rejected (4Q540–541; 4Q548; Milik 1972; Puech 1993; see also Kugler 1996a: 51-52, and note that just because 4Q540–541 were probably not part of *Aramaic Levi* does not mean they played no role in the formation of the Christian *Testament of Levi*; see below).

A pre-Christian, non-Greek 'Testament of Levi' begins to emerge from these sources, to which has been added the addition in the Greek Mt Athos manuscript at *T. Levi* 2.3. Initial attempts to reconstruct such a work relied heavily on the Greek testament's structuring principles (de Jonge 1975c, 1988). The result, of course, is a mostly-Aramaic text that agrees with the Greek testament where material is available (and that usually presumes lost text where there is nothing to match; Kugler 1996a: 28-33 summarizes these attempts). But reconstructing *Aramaic Levi* from the available evidence, without relying on the pattern provided by the Greek testament, produces very different results. *Aramaic Levi* probably began with an account of the Shechem incident (Gen. 34), and continued with Levi's prayer for exaltation to the priesthood. A single vision followed in which Levi is ordained by heavenly angels and instructed on the question of intermarriage. After his vision Levi visited Jacob, who granted him earthly ordination, and Isaac, who instructed him in priestly practice. Then Levi recited his life history and spoke on wisdom and his descendants' future, but at this point the text breaks off. The chart below provides a comparison of this structure for *Aramaic Levi* and the *Testament of Levi*. The versification of *Aramaic Levi* is that of Charles up to the end of the Cairo Geniza material, and for the remaining material it is my own. Elsewhere I provide a full presentation of this reconstruction of *Aramaic Levi* with text, notes and discussion (Kugler 1996a: 61-138; Aschim 1998: 355 correlates my distribution of the Qumran fragments with their numeration in the DJD edition). For an alternative presentation of *Aramaic Levi* based on a different reconstruction of the text, see Greenfield and Stone (1985). The location of the *Aramaic Levi* material in the various sources is indicated in brackets after each entry. The references to Qumran manuscripts in column 2 follow the division imposed on them by the DJD editors.

This reconstruction of *Aramaic Levi* has been greeted with some scepticism (de Jonge 1999; Knibb 1998; less so Aschim 1998), but it remains the only complete proposal that uses all of the available evidence and avoids the prejudice of the Greek testament.

Determining the relationships between the testament, its source(s), and the related tradition in *Jub.* 30.1–32.9 constitutes another problem in the study of the *Testament of Levi*. Debate on the topic is particularly captious. Becker thinks that the testament, the Aramaic work, and *Jubilees* all rely on a common oral tradition (1970: 77-87). Grelot (1956: 402-406), Hultgård (1977: 23-25), Kugler (1996a: 146-55), and VanderKam (1999: 511-18) agree that at least *Jubilees* and *Aramaic Levi* relied on a common Levi apocryphon, but are less certain about the connection between the testament and any of the prior texts. Haupt (1969) deals only with the testament and *Aramaic Levi*, concluding that the testament relied on a work very close to *Aramaic Levi*. De Jonge has said that the Aramaic text, best reconstructed on the model of the Greek testament, probably served as a source for the testament, although its exact form cannot be determined (de Jonge 1999: 89). And Kugel (1993: 52-58) posits a complex set of relationships wherein *Jubilees* relied on a Levi priestly initiation apocryphon and *Aramaic Levi* relied in turn on that apocryphon, a Levi apocalypse, and parts of *Jubilees*; the author of the Greek testament relied on *Aramaic Levi*. This recital of a few of the solutions offered indicates the problem's intractable nature. In the end we can only say confidently that comparison of the testament's contents with the earlier traditions reinforces the conclusion that the *Testaments* included as much Levi material as possible, and that that strategy explains much of the testament's peculiar appearance.

Testament of Levi and Aramaic Levi Compared

Testament of Levi	Aramaic Levi
1.1–2.2—Introduction to the testament.	
2.3-4—Levi tends sheep, reflects on the human condition, and prays for deliverance (cf. *Ar. Levi* supp. 1-19).	
2.5–6.2—Levi dreams, he sees (or hears described) several heavens, his prayer is answered as he is made a priest, and he is commissioned to avenge his sister's rape (cf. *Ar. Levi* supp. 20-27; *Ar. Levi* 4-7).	
6.3–7.4—The sack of Shechem, Jacob's reproach, Levi's self defence.	1-3—The sack of Shechem [Geniza text].
	supp. 1-19—Levi prays (cf. *T. Levi* 2.3-4) [4Q213a; Mt Athos addition at 2.3].
8.1-19—Levi's second vision and a second ordination and elevation to the priesthood, including investi–ture.	supp. 20-27; 4-7—Levi has a vision in which he is elevated to the priesthood and he hears a speech against exogamy [1Q21; 4Q213a].
9.1-5—Travel to Isaac where Isaac blesses Levi, travel to Bethel where Jacob has a vision concerning Levi and appoints him to the priesthood, and travel back to Isaac.	8-12—Travel to Isaac where Isaac blesses Levi, travel to Bethel where Jacob appoints Levi to the priesthood, and travel back to Isaac [4Q213b; Geniza text].
9.6-14—Isaac instructs Levi in cultic matters.	13-61—Isaac instructs Levi in cultic matters [4Q214; 4Q214a; 4Q214b; Geniza text; Mt Athos addition at 18.2].
10.1-5—Levi predicts the fate of his descendants.	
11.1–12.7—Levi narrates his life history.	62-81—Levi narrates his life history [Geniza text; Mt Athos addition at 18.2].
13.1-9—Levi instructs his children on the value of wisdom and learn–ing, and on their relationship to the law of God.	82-101—Levi instructs his children on the value of truth, wisdom and the value of learning [4Q213; 4Q214a; 4Q214b; Geniza text].
14.1–15.4—Levi warns his children regarding their future.	102-106—Levi warns his children regarding their future [4Q213].

In spite of all these uncertainties, many remain ready and willing to speculate about the provenance and aim of a pre-Christian *Testament of Levi* that might have served as the core of a Jewish *Testaments*. For instance, R.H. Charles speculated that the testament at first expressed Pharisaic support for the Hasmoneans (thus the pro-Levi material), but when the Pharisaic community responsible for the *Testaments* grew disenchanted with the Hasmoneans, they introduced the anti-Levi and Judah-as-messiah material into the *Testaments* (Charles 1913: II, 294). In 1956 Pierre Grelot articulated a similar perspective, suggesting that a pre-Christian Levi apocryphon expressed pro-Hasmonean views intended to legitimate the Maccabean merger of the priestly and royal offices. Detlev Haupt (1969), Klaus Beyer (1984, 1994), and, most recently Clemens Thoma (1994), among others, have also suggested that the pre-Christian form the *Testament of Levi* aimed to shore up Hasmonean authority. Anders Hultgård takes the unique view that it was a pro-Zadokite work. He says that it emerged from the Second Temple era trend toward exaltation and 'idealisation of the high priest and the priesthood'. Only later was it given a more universalistic outlook by the addition of passages like *T. Levi* 18 (Hultgård 1980: 94-95). I have suggested that *Aramaic Levi* was a protest against the incumbent priesthood. Its authors were disenchanted with the priests and their failure as intermediaries between God and people. I also suggested that Milik's allusive suggestions of a Samaritan provenance should be given some consideration (Kugler 1996a: 134-38; 1996b). Still others ascribe the pre-Christian *Testament of Levi*, along with the *Testaments* as a whole, to the Essenes (Philonenko 1960; cf. Caquot 1972). Once more, the failure to even approach a consensus signals the improbability of ever achieving one (de Jonge 1988; and Stone 1988a, 1988b offer more restrained observations on the work's possible date and origin). Yet again, we are encouraged to focus our attention on the Christian testament and its meaning, something rightly urged again most recently by Michael Knibb (1998).

However, because it has been so hotly debated, dealing with the question of a purported pre-Christian *Testament of Levi*'s messianism is unavoidable. Many have addressed the question, focusing in particular on *T. Levi* 8; 18. For instance, Charles asserted that *T. Levi* 8.11-15, with its division of Levi's seed into three offices (king, priest and prophet), reflected a pro-Hasmonean anticipation of a king-priest messiah (of whom Charles thought John Hyrcanus was the model; Charles 1913: II, 294; for a sampling of other views: Becker 1970; Caquot 1972; Hultgård 1977: 196-98; Ulrichsen 1991: 196-97). However, the Christian elements in the passage, most especially the claim that the new priesthood would be 'after the fashion of the Gentiles for all the Gentiles', makes any claims for a pre-Christian meaning of the passage unreliable. Hollander and de Jonge (1985: 154) also note that the combination of king, priest and prophet is typically Christian.

At first sight, *T. Levi* 18 provides more promising evidence for pre-Christian messianism in the *Testament of Levi*. Resting squarely on Balaam's oracle (Num. 24.17), the chapter predicts a saviour, a post-levitical high priest (18.2) whose 'star will arise in heaven, as a king' (18.3). From this many conclude that the pre-Christian form of the chapter anticipated a messiah with priestly and royal characteristics, or two separate messiahs (see the wide-ranging treatments of the chapter in Becker 1970: 291-300; Braun 1960; Charles 1908b: 62-67; Chevallier 1958: 126-30; Collins 1995: 92; 1998: 141-42; Haupt 1969: 106-20; Higgins 1966–67: 229-30; Hollander and de Jonge 1985: 177-82; Hultgård 1977: 268-70, 287-90; de Jonge 1986b; Kugler 1996a: 215-16; Lagrange 1931: 122-30; Macky 1969: 336-49; Porter 1949–50: 90-91; Stewart 1967–68: 128-29; Ulrichsen 1991: 204-205; Vawter 1962: 90-92). But for all of the discussion associated with the passage, key elements of its present form make certain that it can be read only as a prediction of Jesus as the ideal high priest and replacement of the levitical line. *Testament of Levi* 18.6-7 clearly refers to Jesus' baptism and 18.9 predicts in typical Christian fashion the magnification of the Gentiles and Israel's decline. So while Christian authors almost certainly relied on a Jewish source that anticipated a priestly (and royal?) messiah (Collins 1995: 92, suggests 4Q541; see discussion above, and Kugler 1996a: 197-98), in its present form *T. Levi* 18 is undeniably a Christian composition (de Jonge 1986b). We cannot be certain that an earlier Jewish version of the chapter proposed two messiahs or a single messiah with priestly and royal characteristics. Likewise, those who see in *T. Levi* 18 evidence that the *Testaments* originated among the authors of the Dead Sea Scrolls are denied their argument (van der Woude 1957; Dupont-Sommer 1953; Philonenko 1960).

Returning finally to the present form of the testament, we first offer brief comments on selected features in the text, reserving for last a discussion of the most pressing issue of all in the study of the *Testament of Levi*, its depiction of Levi and Levites and the relationship between those portraits and the *Testaments'* larger meaning for Jews and Christians.

In the only biographical passage that is obviously connected to a biblical passage (6.3–7.4), Levi recalls his role in the Shechem incident (Gen. 34). In fact, Levi's account depends on Gen. 34 for the general outline of events, but otherwise adds to and adjusts the story vigorously. The authors' reliance on source material surely plays a part here. James Kugel also suggests that an active exegetical imagination is responsible in large measure for some of the more unusual developments of the story (e.g. the claim that Levi killed Shechem, and Simeon slew Hamor [6.4-5]; for more, see Kugel 1992; if Kugel is correct, the exegetical developments almost surely came in the pre-testament stage of the work's development; see also Baarda 1992). In any case, the story seems to function chiefly to exculpate Levi of guilt in the incident, a not unimportant accomplishment in the *Testament of Levi* (see below).

Levi's two visions (2.5–6.2; 8.1-19) set his testament apart from the others, and align it with Naphtali's, which also includes two dream reports (*T. Naph.* 5–6; 7). Most say the double-vision carries over from the *Aramaic Levi* source (e.g. de Jonge 1999). However, I have argued that *Aramaic Levi* probably contained only one vision, and that the second is a creation of the testament's author (Kugler 1996a: 47-59). Whatever their pre-history, the two visions function effectively in the testament's overall strategy of repetition to drive home the point of Levi's exalted status.

The biographical material in the *Testament of Levi* also stands out for its contradiction of other statements in the testament. It also provides evidence of the testament's reliance on some form of *Aramaic Levi*, and for the authors' habit of rearranging the Aramaic material to suit their needs. Levi says in *T. Levi* 12.5 that he was 18 when he slew Shechem, and 19 when he was elevated to the priesthood. But in *T. Levi* 2.2 he says that he was 20 at the time of the Shechem episode, and 4.2-6; 5.2-4 indicate that he was elevated to the priesthood *before* the Shechem incident (6.3-5). Meanwhile, *Ar. Levi* 78 matches *T. Levi* 12.5 almost word for word. So it appears that the authors repeated their source without adjustment in the brief recital of Levi's life history, but in telling *their* version of his story earlier in the testament they adjusted the order of events. Perhaps they placed Levi's elevation to sacerdotal service before the Shechem incident so as to heighten the impression of his intrinsic purity and worthiness before God: a demonstration of his zeal was not necessary for God's choice of him as the chief sacerdotal servant. As we shall see, this would not be surprising in the context of the testament's overall impact.

De Jonge called the cultic instructions in 9.7-14 'a bad extract from a source…which gave Isaac's instructions in a fuller and more readable form' (de Jonge 1953: 40). The source, of course, is *Ar. Levi* 13-61. De Jonge is no doubt correct that *T. Levi* 9.7-14 is an extract from something that closely resembled *Ar. Levi* 13-61. However, it may not be so bad an extract as he thinks. Whereas the Aramaic text only addresses the burnt offering—albeit in detail—the Greek testament informs the reader that Isaac instructed Levi in all forms of sacrifice (9.7; cf. Lev. 7.37). This claim for Levi's comprehensive education in the art of sacrifice is yet another aspect of the testament's portrait of Levi as a complete, ideal priest (Kugler 1996a: 207-209).

The seriatim listing of Levi's life events in 11.1–12.7 is taken over from the Aramaic source as well, but in this case without significant adjustment. Scholarly discussion concerning it has focused chiefly on the chronological indicators in the text (Grelot 1971, 1975, 1981; Wise 1997) and on the material relating to Kohath (see the comments in Greenfield and Stone 1979; see also Baarda 1988, on the peculiarity of the name 'Qehath' in 11.4-6).

The abbreviated parenesis (13.1-9) is striking both for its lack of apparent connection with the rest of the testament and its emphasis on law-keeping, in contrast to the Aramaic text's failure to even mention the word 'law'. The absence of a clear link with other material in the testament is not surprising, since once more we are dealing here with source material. Whether the *Testaments*' authors were the ones who added the word νόμος, we cannot know for certain (see my earlier speculation in Kugler 1996a: 211-12; and de Jonge 1999: 87-88). In any case, the presence of the word clearly advances the *Testaments*' argument. Reference to the law in the *Testaments*, as the earlier survey shows, almost always alludes to the double commandment (see Chapter 1, the 'Main Themes' section). This passage is no different (cf. 13.1, 5). Hence this part of Levi's speech urges the keeping of the law, especially by loving the Lord (13.1-4); love of God leads to right action toward one's neighbour (13.5-6); and right action leads, in turn, to the acquisition of wisdom (13.7-8). Thus the testament takes over the Aramaic source's focus on wisdom and puts it to work to promote good conduct through adherence to the law (for others on this passage, see especially H.W. Hollander 1981: 57-62; Küchler 1979: 491-99; Philonenko 1979, and the discussion of the passage in Chapter 3 below).

That the S.E.R. pattern is thrice-repeated in *T. Levi* 10; 14–16 has also attracted a great deal of attention. Various explanations involving compositional stages and multiple sources have been offered to solve the apparent problem (for example, Ulrichsen 1991: 197-202, and the literature cited therein), but de Jonge certainly has the better of all commentators on this point. Noting the general repetitiveness in the testament (cf. 2.9-12 and 4.2-6; 2-5 and 8), he suggests that the S.E. pattern is repeated three times to emphasise that the sons of Levi, 'notwithstanding their firm commitment in 19.1-3…will not be faithful in the teaching and administration of the law' (1981: 520), and that they will rebel against the saviour. The R. portion of the S.E.R. pattern, appearing in its complete form only in ch. 16, promises that in spite of these things the saviour will return even for their salvation. As we shall see, this fits well in the overall plan and aim of the testament.

The seven jubilee history of the priesthood in 17.1-11 also draws its share of attention (for example, Otzen 1953, sees in ch. 17 a history of the Aaronite priesthood; Milik 1972, takes the view that the chapter is an apocalypse; compare Dupont-Sommer 1951–52). Yet another source of undetermined origin, it is also well-suited to the purposes of the *Testaments'* authors. Its story of the levitical priesthood's decline fits in with the testament's overall indictment of Levi's descendants. It also serves as the prelude to the priesthood's renewal in the advent of the non-levitical saviour and high priest of 18.1-14 (see discussion above).

Finally, the shift from third person address to first person plural in 19.2-3 receives some attention. Slingerland (1984) claims this as one of the 'levitical hallmarks' of the *Testaments*, but he offers little more than this to support his view that the work comes from levitical circles (cf. Hultgård). More persuasive is de Jonge's suggestion that the reference highlights the authors' embrace of the early Christian premise that the Christian community constituted God's 'true highpriestly race' (de Jonge 1988: 385, citing Justin, *Dial.* 116.3); thus they assume the role of Levi's descendants, affirming their own priestly role.

Apart from these and some other smaller items of interest (for example, the early Christian theme of the torn temple veil in 10.3 [cf. *T. Benj.* 9.4; Mt. 27.51]; Hollander and de Jonge 1985: 79-81), the most pressing interpretative issue is understanding the testament's conflicting portraits of Levi and his descendants. Why does the testament describe Levi as the most exalted priest of all (2.10; 4.2-4a; 5.2a; 8.2-17; 9.3; cf. 10.2a) and his descendants as rapacious and violent sacerdotalists (10.2c-3; 14.5-8; 16.1-2; 17.4-9, 11) who lose their office because of their corruption (4.4a; 5.2b; 8.14; 18.1-2)? Why do Levi's descendants take such a prominent role in rejecting Jesus (4.4b; 10.2b; 14.2-4; 16.3)? And why do they nevertheless participate in the joyful exaltation at Jesus' advent (16.5; 18.14)? Answering these questions addresses the relationship of the *Testament of Levi* to the *Testaments* as a whole.

The testament's title, 'about priesthood and arrogance', provides the first piece of evidence for solving the puzzle. That the testament deals with the priesthood is obvious, but the term 'arrogant', ὑπερήφανος, appears only in *T. Levi* 17.11. In fact, one suspects that 'arrogance' is actually a gratuitous addition made convenient by the fact that the preceding testament is concerned with 'envy', a vice closely allied with arrogance in the Graeco-Roman imagination. But the convenience is also fortuitous in that 'arrogance' nicely covers the reasons that Levi's descendants, the heirs of Levi's priesthood, could go so wrong in the practice of their office and become the chief adversaries of God's redeemer. In their arrogance they lead Israel astray (10.2c-3) by cultic neglect and misdemeanours (14.5, 8; 16.1) and by failing as teachers and interpreters of the law (14.6; 16.2). It was their pride that led them, in turn, to rebel against the messiah (14.1-2, 7).

Meanwhile, the biographical, parenetic and future-oriented sections underscore God's choice of Levi for the priesthood and Levi's reputation for exercising his office honourably. By retelling the Shechem episode the authors remove from Levi all culpability (6.3–7.4). Levi's zeal at Shechem won him the privilege of visions and tours of the heavens and threefold investiture in the priestly office (2.4–6.2; 8.1–9.6). And Isaac's general, but nearly comprehensive cultic instructions for Levi further prove Levi's correctness as God's first priest (9.7-14). Levi's brief exhortation also emphasizes his transcendent grasp of the priestly office's importance, and links him to the *Testaments'* larger agenda of connecting the double commandment with good conduct in general (13.1-9, especially vv. 1, 5). The S.E.R. passages (10; 14-16) clear Levi of all responsibility for his descendants' actions. *T. Levi* 10.2 assures the reader that the descendants' misdeeds are their own, not Levi's. And the priesthood finally comes to an end because of the subsequent generations' sins, never because of any of Levi's actions (17.1–18.1). In short, Levi exemplifies all that a priest should be, and all that the saviour with priestly characteristics will be (*T. Levi* 18.1-14).

Thus the tribe rejoices at the end of time in spite of its corruption and its rejection of the messiah because of Levi and his adherence to the law, his ability to keep God's commandments, and his theological insight. *T. Levi* 18.14 joins Levi to Abraham, Isaac and Jacob, for whose sake the *Testaments* say God will give even the lawless of Israel a second chance through the return of the messiah (*T. Levi* 15.4; *T. Ash.* 7.7). Thus the *Testaments* elevate Levi to the same status as his father, grandfather and great-grandfather (cf. 4Q225 2 ii 11-12 and 4Q226 7.4 [4QPsJub[a, b]] for a similar listing the four together). This also provides him with sufficient significance in God's sight to merit even for his corrupt descendants multiple chances at God's mercy. Levi, the father of a tribe of apostate priests, is also that tribe's redeeming grace before the God of mercy.

The latter statement captures the relationship between this testament and the rest of the patriarchs' speeches. The dynamic between the law-abiding and theologically insightful patriarch and his corrupt, saviour-rejecting descendants epitomizes the *Testaments'* agenda: to offer through the instruction and predictions of the patriarchs proof of God's undying will to secure Israel's fate. Even when the other tribes, like Levi's, fail to heed their ancestors' advice, God will provide another chance at salvation through the return of the saviour. Moreover, the portrait of Levi as priest gives insight into the priestly nature of the messiah whom God sends to fulfil his will.

Testament of Judah

Judah's long speech is easily summarized. He addresses the title topics, 'courage' (ἀνδρεία), 'love of money' (φιλαργυρία) and 'impurity' (πορνεία) throughout the biographical and ethical sections (1.1–20.5). But when his attention shifts to the future, the focus also shifts to the royal line that will come from his seed and eventually produce a saviour for Israel (21.1–24.6; compare 1.3-6; 15.1-6; 17.5, passages that foreshadow the theme of kingship). This redeemer will reward the faithful with resurrection from the dead (25.1-5).

The material in *T. Jud.* 2.1–7.11; 9.1-8, on Judah's courage, seems out of place because it lacks any connection to the hortatory material in 13.1–20.5 (although Judah's contradictory aside at the start of the parenesis condemning boastfulness about one's youthful strength [13.2b] fumblingly attempts to integrate this material with the ethical section). That most of it closely parallels other known texts probably explains its presence and the testament's additional focus on courage. Indeed, the abundant source material in Levi's and Naphtali's testaments prove that the authors of the *Testaments* were inveterate collectors of traditions regarding the patriarchs. In this case traditions about Judah's battles with Canaanites (3.1–7.11) and his valour in a war against Esau and his sons (9.1-8) reflect the known source material.

The material on Judah's courage begins by reporting on his gallantry as a hunter (2.1-7). The description of Judah's energetic pursuit of various kinds of animals (deer, horses, lions, bears, boars and oxen) recalls David's daring defence of his flock (cf. *T. Jud.* 2.4a and 1 Sam. 17.34-36; compare Sir. 47.3; Syriac Psalm of David [151A] 3 [Charlesworth 1985] [cf. *T. Gad* 1.3]) and Samson's slaughter of a lion (cf. *T. Jud.* 2.4b and Judg. 14.6). Philonenko (1970) suggests an additional connection with Heracles' courage in the animal world (Apollodorus, *The Library* II.5.1-8 [Frazier]). Perhaps by this vignette the testament's creators, in the interest of demonstrating the coherence of biblical, Jewish and Christian teaching with the norms of the dominant culture, intentionally linked Judah to a biblical hero, David, and to Herakles, a popular figure in Graeco-Roman mythology. But ironically Herakles was thought to have won 'immortality through suffering and overcoming the passions' (Ferguson 1993: 149, n. 11), certainly not something Judah (or David) achieved, as the rest of the testament proves.

The remaining material concerning Judah's courage, as noted above, parallels other known texts. The widely-attested tale of Judah's exploits against the Canaanites in *T. Jud.* 3.1–7.11 develops from Jacob's dying gift

to Joseph of a larger portion of land than his brothers received, the land
that Jacob 'took from the hand of the Amorites' by force (Gen. 48.22; cf.
Jub. 34.1-9; *Midrash Wayissa'u* [=*Chronicle of Yerahmeel* 36]; *Book of Yashar*
[Hollander and de Jonge 1985: 451-56]). Meanwhile, the story of Judah's
role in the war with Esau and his sons in *T. Jud*. 9.1-8 has no biblical
basis but does parallel *Jub*. 37.1–38.14 (*Midrash Wayissa'u* [=*Chronicle of
Yerahmeel* 37]; *Book of Yashar* [Hollander and de Jonge 1985: 451-56]).
VanderKam wryly observes that the parallel accounts 'offer a splendid
example of a mushrooming story' (1977: 218-19 n. 23). But in which
direction did the story grow? The number of opinions on the topic nearly
matches the number of commentators who have taken it up. For
instance, while Hultgård (1982: 123-27) suggests that *T. Jud*. 3.1–7.11
abbreviates a longer account of the war with the Canaanites, Becker
(1970: 114-25) thinks that we can only speak of an oral tradition that was
used by a number of authors. In fact, because of the substantial differences among them—and lacking the benefit of earlier evidence such as
we have in the Qumran manuscripts of *Aramaic Levi*—one despairs of settling the relationships among the various witnesses. The most one can
say is that the *Testaments*, true to form, took up and used available sources,
this time to address the question of Judah's courage.

The rest of the biographical section attends to the other themes
announced in the testament's title by expanding on Gen. 38 (this material
lacks parallels in extrabiblical texts, although some detect echoes in *Jub*.
41; Hollander and de Jonge 1985: 186). After reporting his defeat of the
Canaanites and before recounting his war with Esau, Judah briefly introduces his wife, Bathshua (8.1-3). The full story of how he came to marry
Bathshua, a Canaanite, and how Tamar, his daughter-in-law seduced
him, comes out in 10.1–12.12. Judah blames his ill-chosen marriage and
incestuous encounter on the intoxicating effect of wine and alluring
women, and on Bathshua's uncooperative nature. Bathshua's wealth and
adornment-aided beauty lured him into calamitous matrimony (11.1-2;
13.4-7; 14.6; 17.1). Bathshua's spiteful advice to her sons against
procreative intercourse with Tamar (because Tamar was not a fellow
Canaanite; 11.3-6) led to Tamar's predicament and her solution
involving Judah. And Judah's drunkenness and concomitant submission
to lustful passion led to his intercourse with Tamar (12.3, 6). Throughout Judah fails to acknowledge his responsibility in the difficulties that
befell him and his sons, blaming them instead on the power that wine,
women and his passions had over him.

Judah's dodge, however, is hardly surprising, for the *Testaments'* treatment of women agrees with a common Hellenistic conception of the
feminine gender: she is often intent on gaining power over a man's

wealth and power through wile and allure, and the same qualities trigger a man's self-destructive passions (Walcot 1988: 1283-86; cf. *T. Reub.* 5.1-4; on the connection of the latter passage with *T. Jud.* 12.3 in particular, see Wassén 1994). For instance, while Tamar has a significantly reduced role in this account as compared to Gen. 38, she does function as the trickster responsible in large part for Judah's indiscretion! By contrast, the testament tells us a great deal about Bathshua, Judah's wife, but only to put her in a negative light as well. She only wins Judah's hand through wine, adornment and the allure of her father's wealth. She opposes Tamar's marriage to Judah's sons. She instructs Er and Onan not to impregnate Tamar. And she, not Judah, prohibits Shelah's marriage to Tamar.

Judah's view that wine without moderation gives women, wealth, lust and greed free reign over men appears again in the parenesis in 13.1–19.4 (note as well the repeated reference to Judah's violation of the law in marrying Bathshua, a Canaanite in 13.7; 14.6; cf. Gen. 24.3; 28.6, 8). Judah warns against inebriation, the allure of women and the temptations of wealth (13.1–14.8; 16.1–19.4), saying that the loss of self-control to all three results in the loss of one's kingship (15.1-6). At this critical juncture he also remarks, in keeping with the *Testaments*' focus on the two commandments, that impurity and love of money lead to evil against one's neighbour and dishonourable conduct toward God (18.3, 5-6).

In 20.1-5 Judah completes the parenesis with a passage that has been described as unexpected (Hollander and de Jonge 1985: 219). But in fact it functions to integrate Judah's moral exhortation into the *Testaments*' larger claim that virtue comes from God's guidance. Judah observes that two spirits, one of truth and one of deceit, pursue the human soul. Comparison with similar passages (*T. Ash.* 6.4-6; *T. Benj.* 6.1) indicates that the human under God's care lives in the spirit of truth, and ascendancy of the spirit of deceit signals Beliar's power over the person.

The first of Judah's future predictions, an L.J. passage (21.1-6a), generates considerable interest among commentators for a number of reasons. First, in 21.2, 4a Judah announces the dominion of the priestly office over the crown, and second, in 21.4b scholars discern a polemic against the Hasmoneans ('priesthood [is] higher than the kingship on earth unless it falls away from the Lord through sin'). Thus some think that the passage provides evidence of a pre-Christian *Testament of Judah*, and indicates that it originated in the Hasmonean period as a pro-priestly, anti-Hasmonean treatise (Collins 1995: 90). While that may be true, in its present condition it points to the priority of the saviour's mediatorial character.

The shift to second person singular address in 21.5-6a also arouses interest. As in *T. Iss.* 5.4-8, where the same shift in address also occurs, the speaker could be God addressing the patriarch, or the patriarch could be speaking to his tribe as a collective singular. The latter seems the most likely.

The following material, 21.6–23.5 (an S.E.R passage), twice describes the rise, fall and restoration of Judah's kingship (21.6–22.3; 23.1-5). In both accounts Judah's credibility is established by his *vaticinia ex eventu* allusions to well-known royal abuses, actions not unconnected to Judah's own vices (cf., for example, 21.7 and 1 Sam. 8.10-18; 23.2 and Hos. 4.13-14; it is not necessary to speculate about Hasmonean-era meanings for this text as does Hultgård 1977: 145). Consequently the reader is prepared for the elaboration of the R. element of 23.1-5 in *T. Jud.* 24.1-6.

Testament of Judah 24.1-6 draws at least as much attention as *T. Levi* 18 because of its comparable significance for understanding the *Testaments'* messianism and possible pre-Christian form (see the discussions with bibliography in Becker 1970: 319-23; Ulrichsen 1991: 174). By analogy with *T. Levi* 18, some think 24.1-3 originally identified the star from Balaam's oracle (Num. 24.17) as a levitical messiah ('from my [Judah's] seed' in 24.1 is taken as a later addition), and 24.4-6 linked the sceptre with a royal messiah from Judah (Charles 1913: II, 323; Hultgård 1977: 204-13; see the discussion of this passage in Collins 1995: 91-92; note also Nickelsburg and Stone 1983: 170-71, who think the passage expects two messiahs). Others use the dual messianism of such a hypothetical, reconstructed Jewish text to link the *Testaments* to the people of the scrolls (van der Woude 1957: 205). But de Jonge (1953: 89-90) points out that no matter its earlier forms, the chapter as we have it now is undeniably Christian. De Jonge is certainly correct: 24.1-6 is nothing more or less than a Christian prophecy of Jesus, a redeemer endowed with priestly and royal traits. Among other things, the connection between *T. Jud.* 24.2-3 and Jesus' baptism certainly suggests this conclusion (compare *T. Levi* 18.6-8).

Before giving the standard conclusion in 26.1-4 Judah predicts the resurrection of the patriarchs after the messiah's appearance (25.1-5). Notably, the order of resurrection after Abraham, Isaac and Jacob begins with Levi and continues with Judah, Joseph, Benjamin, Simeon and Issachar, and then continues from there 'in order' (25.1). The list of the first six patriarchs depends on Deut. 27.12, but the adjusted order also reflects the *Testaments'* special interest in Levi, Judah, Joseph and Benjamin. And placing Levi first among those who follow Abraham, Isaac and Jacob may also reflect the *Testaments'* predilection for associating Levi with the 'senior' ancestors (cf. *T. Levi* 18.14; 4Q225 2 ii 11-12; 4Q226 7.4, cited above at the end of the section on *Testament of Levi*; for an explanation of the curious order in 25.2, see Hollander and de Jonge 1985: 230).

Like Levi's speech, Judah's address is pivotal for the *Testaments'* capacity to communicate the nature of God's abiding interest in Israel's fate. It pursues an ethical agenda—avoidance of the vices of lust and greed—and subsumes the specifics of ethical conduct to keeping God's commandments to love God and one's neighbour. And the testament reveals through the trustworthy words of the patriarch the identity of God's redeemer for Israel: he is above all the priestly mediator between heaven and earth (*T. Jud.* 22.3b-4; 24.2) and secondarily a royal descendant from the line of Judah.

Testament of Issachar

Issachar's testament shifts attention to the virtue of 'simplicity', ἁπλότης. After narrating the circumstances surrounding his conception and birth (1.3–2.5), Issachar devotes the rest of his autobiographical comments to describing the value of a farmer's simple life (3.1-8; 7.2-6). Thus the virtue of simplicity and the agrarian life, themes often connected in Hellenistic thought, pair up in the story of an exemplary patriarch. Issachar's exhortations urge his children to lead a similarly simple life (4.1–5.3), and his future predictions mostly speak of the evil that comes from departing from simplicity and the good that its pursuit yields (5.4-8; 6.1-4). 7.1, 7-8 provide a typical conclusion, apart from the intervention of more autobiography in vv. 2-6.

Noticing the disparate material included in the report on the circumstances of Issachar's conception and birth in *T. Iss.* 1.3–2.5, Becker suggests that it grew in stages (1970: 335-36). However the account reads well as a unity and requires no redactional history to explains its peculiarities. They probably result instead from the authors' use of a variety of extrabiblical elements to promote sexual continence, a topic nicely placed on the heels of Judah's testament and its focus on restraining lust.

The testament adjusts the biblical story of Issachar's conception in several ways. In Gen. 30.14-18 Issachar was conceived because of Reuben's discovery of mandrakes, their delivery to his mother Leah, and Rachel's bargaining away a night with Jacob in exchange for them. The testament changes the story by having Rachel take the mandrakes from Reuben before he can deliver them to his mother (1.3). Reuben's wailing at this injustice brings Leah on the scene (1.4). Rachel withholds the mandrakes because she wants them in place of the children she does not have (1.6). The number of mandrakes is set at two (1.7), and from there the bargaining for Jacob's bed begins. Rachel offers Jacob to Leah for a night in exchange for the fruit (1.8). Relying on facts known from Gen. 29.15-30 Leah retorts by reminding Rachel that she is only Jacob's second wife, while Leah is the 'wife of his youth' (1.9). Rachel's soliloquy in response reminds Leah that it was only the injustice done between men (Laban and Jacob) that put her second (1.10-13). Then Rachel offers one night for one mandrake, on account of which Issachar is conceived (1.14-15). The next unit develops from Gen. 30.19-24. An angel comes to Jacob to explain that because she chose 'continence', ἐγκράτεια, over intercourse, Rachel will finally bear two children. For that reason (and presumably because she wished for intercourse and not continence) Leah's quota of children was reduced from eight to six (2.1-3). Finally, proving her continence, Rachel gives up a second night with Jacob to Leah in exchange for the remaining mandrake, which she dedicates to God (2.4-5).

De Jonge (1953: 78-80) draws attention to a parallel, but contrasting two-mandrakes-for-sex story in *Gen. Rab.* 72.3, 5. The rabbis indicate that God was pleased with Leah for forfeiting the mandrakes to provide children to Jacob, so she was rewarded with two more tribes from her womb beyond the four she had already. Meanwhile, Rachel earned God's displeasure for her willingness to give up Jacob for the fruit, so she lost two tribes promised to her, ending up with only two. De Jonge suggests, probably correctly, that the *Testaments'* authors knew the rabbinic tale and reversed it to give expression to the early Christian, Hellenistic-Jewish and Graeco-Roman attitudes toward marital sexuality (see the citations of texts from all three traditions in de Jonge 1990, and the discussion of sexual restraint in the section on the *Testament of Reuben* above). Thus this convoluted passage contributes to the *Testaments'* implicit claim that Jews and Christians could live by the standards of the Graeco-Roman world while satisfying their religious obligations.

The dual focus on Issachar's simplicity and his role as a farmer in 3.1-8 prompts some to speculate that the material concerning one or the other is secondary (Becker 1970: 336-39). Such speculation is unnecessary. Genesis 49.15 LXX provided the notion that Issachar was a farmer, and Cynic–Stoic thought linked the virtue of simplicity to the pastoralist's life. Capitalizing on that, and on Judaism's and Christianity's appreciation of the virtue of simplicity, the *Testaments'* authors simply made the connection on their own (3.1-4). They even link this passage with the preceding reflections on continence by having Issachar say that the hardworking life of a simple farmer gave him no time or energy to contemplate women, let alone dally with them in sexual frivolity (3.5). As to the rewards for simplicity, Issachar realized them richly, both in the doubling of his goods and in his natural inclination toward generosity and piety (3.6-8).

Also in connection with the biography, it is worth noting that the authors of the *Testaments* almost certainly knew, but declined to use, another tradition, developed from 1 Chron. 12.32, that Issachar's tribe excelled in study of the Torah. That tradition would hardly have served the *Testaments* in identifying piety with Graeco-Roman standards of conduct (Eppel 1930: 147-53, also claims that simplicity is the central virtue of the *Testaments*; cf. H.W. Hollander 1981: 10).

Issachar's parenesis naturally follows his autobiographical comments (4.1–5.3). He counsels singleness of heart and simplicity, because God takes pleasure in it (4.1). Issachar defines simplicity as being happy with what one has and trusting in God for all else (4.2-6). But the bottom line, says Issachar, is obedience to the law of God by keeping the double commandment to love the Lord and one's neighbour (5.1-2). Thus Issachar, like his older brothers, upholds the *Testaments*' claim that salvation rests in love of God and neighbour, and that doing those two things fulfils the virtues required by the ancestors.

The first future-oriented passage, 5.4-8, presents a number of difficulties. The shift to second person singular address in the blessing of 5.4-5 is peculiar. As in *T. Jud.* 21.5-6a, the speaker could be God addressing the patriarch, or the patriarch could be addressing his children as a collective. If the latter suggestion is correct, than 5.6 ('because our father Jacob blessed me with the blessings of the earth and first fruits') is 'the ground for the earlier blessing' (Hollander and de Jonge 1985: 247).

A second oddity in 5.4-8 is the pairing of Issachar with Abel (5.4). Of course, by comparison with Gen. 4 a more logical pairing on the basis of profession could be made between Cain and Issachar. However, Hollander and de Jonge (1985: 247) gather impressive evidence from Jewish and Christian authors that Abel had become a paradigm of simplicity and honour in Jewish and Christian imagination (see, for example, Josephus, *Ant.* 1.52-59 [Thackeray *et al.*]). Thus the identification actually makes good sense, and provides further indication of the *Testaments*' liberal embrace of widespread Jewish and Christian *topoi*.

While the L.J. passage in 5.7 is uncomplicated, 5.8 provides another puzzle in this section. A reference to Gad follows the benedictions for Issachar, Levi and Judah, indicating that he is 'to destroy the bands that come against Israel' (5.8; cf. Gen. 49.19 LXX). Although the reference is suited to Gad, there is no clear reason for his appearance at this point.

After a typical S.E.R. passage (6.1-4; abandoning simplicity is equated with forsaking the commandments and cleaving to Beliar [6.1-2]), 7.1, 8-9 gives the standard conclusion for a testament. Issachar's declaration of innocence (7.2-7) breaks into the middle of this finale. In many ways his litany summarizes the *Testaments* to this point. It lists among the sins that

Issachar did not commit many of the misdeeds of Reuben, Simeon, Levi's children and Judah (7.2-4, 5b; lust, covetousness [envy?], theft, drunkenness, and deceit). His chief righteousness, on the other hand, was his fulfilment of the all-important double command to love the Lord and his neighbour (7.6). Doing this, says Issachar, keeps the spirits of Beliar and of human dominion from you, and gives you power over the wild beasts (cf. *T. Jud.* 2.1-7). Issachar's declaration not only recalls much of what has already come to light through the other testaments. It also proves that the patriarchs' advice can be kept, and that heeding two simple commandments, to love God and to love one's neighbour, is at the heart of God-pleasing virtue. Thus Issachar's speech surely is a 'typical testament' (de Jonge 1975d: 291-315). In this respect it is noteworthy that Issachar's speech contributes nothing to the messianism of the *Testaments*. According to Issachar, Israel's fate depends above all on keeping God's commandments.

Testament of Zebulun

Zebulun's speech addresses compassion and mercy. It includes two unrelated biographical passages, one concerning Zebulun's compassion on the occasion of the sale of Joseph (1.4–4.13), and a second on his mercy as a fisherman and shepherd (5.5–7.4). Zebulun's exhortations are scattered among the biographical accounts. He encourages his children to lead compassionate lives as he did (5.1-4; 7.2-3; 8.1-3). His predictions focus on his descendants' failure to heed his advice and on the historical and eschatological rewards and punishments that will come to the obedient and the disobedient (9.1–10.7). This testament adds especially to the *Testaments'* argument the notion that the messiah embodies the virtues counselled by the ancestors.

The *Testament of Zebulun* presents special text-critical problems. Apart from a few fragmentary phrases, the Armenian and Slavonic versions and Greek manuscripts *eafchij* lack 6.4–8.3, and parts of 8.4, 6; 9.5, 6, 8. Some claim that the missing portions are actually later additions to an earlier, shorter testament (Becker 1970: 203-13; Ulrichsen 1991: 92-101). De Jonge notes, however, that without the material in the longer version only 5.1 and 9.7 address the theme of compassion; thus it is more likely that later scribes shortened the text to 'avoid some of the more extravagant examples of Zebulun's compassion' (Hollander and de Jonge 1985: 254; see also de Jonge [ed.] 1975: 144-60).

After an introduction that dates his speech two years after Joseph's death (1.1-3), Zebulun declares his innocence (as did Issachar at the end of his speech; 7.2-7). Zebulun acknowledges, however, that he did fail to tell Jacob of Joseph's sale (1.4-5). Thus Zebulun's testament sets out from the start to confirm, as did Issachar's, that virtue can be achieved.

In the first biographical unit Zebulun recalls the sale of Joseph (2.1–4.13; cf. Gen. 37). He adds to the biblical account numerous details that serve his aim of promoting compassion and of condemning envy, anger and hatred. Thus Simeon and Gad, exemplars of envy and hatred, were the chief aggressors against Joseph and the reason that Judah feared for Joseph's life (2.1; 4.2b, 11-13). Joseph uttered a pitiful plea to his brothers for compassion and mercy because he had committed no sin against them (2.2-3; see the brothers' curious comment in Gen. 42.21 that they did not listen to Joseph's plea when they sold him; this comment in the testament seems to provide the plea itself). Zebulun's empathy and compasssion for Joseph were so great that he wept with Joseph, shielded him from his brothers, and refused to eat (along with Judah) when the others supped (2.4-6; 4.2a; by contrast, Reuben's futile pursuit of the merchants with the proceeds from the sale of Joseph [4.5-7a] arose from his anxiety about what he would tell Jacob).

The testament takes up an intricate exegetical tradition in an excursus on what the brothers (excluding Zebulun) did with the proceeds from Joseph's sale. The passage underscores the testament's claim that those without compassion and mercy suffer grave consequences (3.1-8; cf. *Targ. Ps.-J.* Gen. 37.28 [Maher]). Zebulun builds on Amos 2.6, saying that rather than purchase food with the blood money, the brothers bought sandals to tread Joseph underfoot and to avoid 'eating of their brother'. Their reason for 'treading him underfoot' was to repudiate his claim that he would rule over them (3.1-3; cf. Gen. 37.5-8). In 3.4-8 Zebulun links his brothers' action to the punishment for refusing to perform the law of levirate marriage (Deut 25.9-10; in 3.4, however, the practice is attributed to Enoch since the events take place before the law of Moses is given), because by doing this to Joseph they wished to refuse him any offspring. So God brought them to Egypt, where God made them do obeisance before their brother, an act that required them to remove their footwear (3.6; cf. Gen. 43.24 and the implicit removal of the brothers' sandals to have their feet washed) and endure the spit of the Egyptians (3.7).

Other additions to the biblical account of Joseph's sale focus on Joseph alone. That God prevented water from flooding the pit while Joseph occupied it (2.8) fits the *Testaments'* theme of God's protection for Joseph. And that Joseph is said to have languished in the pit for three days and three nights is almost certainly meant to make him a type of Jesus (de Jonge 1960: 204; compare also the reference to the price of Joseph's blood [3.3] with Mt. 27.6; Argyle 1955–56).

The second biographical unit concerns Zebulun's compassion and mercy as a fisherman and shepherd (5.5–7.4). His seafaring reputation derives from Gen. 49.13 LXX (cf. *Gen. Rab.* 72.5; 99.9 [Neusner]; *Targ. Ps.-J.* Gen. 49.13 [Maher]; note also Zebulun's claim to have invented sailing because God gave him the necessary 'understanding and wisdom', σύνεσιν καὶ σοφίαν; Kee 1978: 263, suggests that this echoes the Stoic view of humanity). However, the *Testaments*' authors almost certainly provided his profession as a fisherman. Relying on Deut. 33.19, tradition normally depicts Zebulun as a merchant; but to avoid the unsavoury overtones of such an occupation, the authors of the testament made him a fisherman, a profession that the ancient imagination likened to that of the farmer and his virtuous simplicity (see the discussion and literature cited in Hollander and de Jonge 1985: 266). Zebulun's winter occupation as a shepherd was likewise probably chosen because of its association with simplicity (see the discussion above of the mention of Abel in *T. Iss.* 5.4). The testament discusses both pastimes to prove again Zebulun's compassion and mercy for others (6.4-5, 7; 7.1, 4), to cite the rewards God gave him for his kindness (5.5; 6.6), and to encourage similar virtue in his children (7.2-3).

The parenesis in the *Testament of Zebulun* underscores the last two points in reverse order. Zebulun admonishes his sons to be compassionate and merciful in their dealings, and cites his and their health in contrast to his brothers' and their sons' sickness as evidence that God rewards the kind and punishes the wicked (5.1-4). From this he draws the conclusion that God, who comes to earth as embodied compassion (8.2; cf. 9.8), will reside with those who exhibit the same quality (8.3). Adding to Joseph's glorification and his own, Zebulun supports his claim that compassion has empathy for compassion by noting that Joseph, a man of mercy, had special compassion for Zebulun when he and his brothers went to Egypt for food (8.4; cf. Gen. 50.15). Thus his sons should emulate Joseph as well.

An exhortation to unity (9.1-4) introduces Zebulun's predictions of the future. It also leads him to say that his descendants' failure to take his advice regarding unity will lead to the division of Israel under two kings, abominable religious practices (9.5), and captivity among the Gentiles (9.6). Philonenko (1960: 5) takes this to refer to the dispute between Hyrcanus II and Aristobulus II and Rome's subsequent take-over. However, the passage more obviously refers to the division of the kingdom after Solomon (1 Kgs 12). Thus the restoration after Israel's repentance in 9.7 refers to the return from exile, and 9.8 refers to the coming of the messiah in compassion, followed by the descendants' renewed sin in rejection of him (9.9). As he concludes his speech Zebulun urges his children not to be disquieted (10.1), for the certainty of his own future resurrection proves that regardless of one's response to the messiah's appearance, those who have been compassionate and merciful—'who have kept the law of the Lord and the commandments of Zebulun their father'—will share in the rejoicing at the end of days (10.2). As for those who fail, they shall suffer great punishment (10.3).

The *Testament of Zebulun* adds compassion and mercy to the list of virtues that God will reward with salvation. Moreover, it demonstrates that these are precisely the qualities God exhibits for God's people, especially in the messiah. The speech makes it equally clear that God provides compassion and mercy, even through the messiah, especially for those who have exhibited those qualities toward others (8.2-3; 9.7-8). Thus Zebulun's address implies that the messiah confirms the standards set out by the patriarchs (cf. *T. Levi* 16.3a). His speech also substantiates the significance of keeping the double commandment for achieving salvation-earning virtue.

Testament of Dan

Dan's speech ostensibly addresses the evils of anger and lying, although he focuses principally on anger, θυμός (the word itself appears in 1.8; 2.2, 4; 3.1, 4, 5; 4.1, 2, 3, 6, 7; 5.1; 6.8; lying turns up in 2.4; 3.6; 4.6, 7; 5.1; 6.8 and is almost always merely an adjunct of anger). Dan describes anger's all-consuming power over the human soul. The structure of Dan's testament differs somewhat from the norm. In an unusual arrangement after the standard opening formula (1.1-2), Dan introduces parenesis (1.3) before giving a brief autobiographical account (1.4-9). He returns to exhortation in 2.1–5.3, calling his children to avoid anger and lying, and concludes his testament with unusually complex future predictions (5.4-13; 6.2b-7, 11) intermixed with further exhortation (6.1-2a, 8-10). All in all, this testament especially advances the *Testaments'* argument by strengthening the connections between Graeco-Roman standards of conduct, the ancestors' teaching, and the example of God's saviour, Jesus.

Dan's story of anger against Joseph and his near attempt on Joseph's life has no obvious biblical basis. However, it is true that Danites appear mostly in a negative light in the Hebrew Bible (Charles 1908b: 128-29; Whitelam 1992: 11). The blasphemer of Lev. 24.11 was born of a Danite mother married to an Egyptian, Danites refused to fight against Sisera (Judg. 5.17), and they are described as thieves and idolaters (Judg. 18.1-31; 1 Kgs 12.29). Likewise, the targumic tradition treats Dan with disdain (*Targ. Ps.-J.* Deut. 25.18 [Clarke], cited in Charles 1908b: 129), and he and Gad are the aggressors against Aseneth in *Jos. Asen.* 24-28 (Burchard

1985). But the Danite Samson provides the most fruitful connection between Dan's testament and one of his biblical descendants. Samson's anger also leads to troubles and violence (Judg. 14.19), yet like Dan, he has redeeming features that permit him a vestige of dignity and authority (for more on the echoes of Samson in the *Testament of Dan*, see Chapter 3).

In any event, the biographical material links Dan with the vice of anger, and establishes from the beginning the unusual intensity of the human emotion. While other patriarchs speak of their vices as past obsessions, when he says that he rejoiced at Joseph's death Dan hints that his vice governed a part of his soul even in his latter years (1.4; note also the language in the same verse idealizing Joseph as 'a true and good man'). Dan reports that years before he felt the same pleasure when he and his brothers sold Joseph because Jacob's greater love of Joseph had made him jealous, ζῆλος (1.5-6; cf. φθόνος in 2.5 and the similarly synonymous use of both words in *Testament of Simeon*). Foreshadowing the testament's claim that Satan controls Dan's tribe, Dan then notes that a spirit of Beliar spoke to him directly to suggest an attempt on Joseph's life (1.7). But in keeping with God's special protection for Joseph, Dan's attempt fails for lack of a victim, since his brothers had already sold Joseph (1.9).

Besides urging his children to avoid anger and lying (1.3; 2.1; 5.1-3), Dan uses his exhortation to instruct his children on the nature and effects of rage. In doing so his instruction underscores the affiliation that the patriarchs' teaching shares with Graeco-Roman philosophical notions while strengthening the theological roots of the patriarchs' parenesis. Like the classical moralists, Dan understands that the power of an angry man is actually enhanced by the emotion (3.2b-5), but that anger unchecked can overtake life and unbalance reason (2.1–3.2a; 4.1-7; cf. Plutarch, *Moralia* 453F-454B [Babbitt *et al.*]; see also the kinship of Dan's advice not to be provoked to anger by an ill-spoken word or deluded by praise with the general Cynic–Stoic encouragement to stand above external influences on one's emotions). But Dan theologizes these insights by attributing the spirit of anger to Satan (3.6; cf. 5.6; 6.1, which also use the name 'Satan' for 'Beliar'), and by advising that escape from anger and Satan come only through flight to God and compliance with the double commandment to love God and neighbour (5.1-3). Notably, Charles (1908b: 127) and Becker (1974: 94) insist that 5.3 is the first known combination of Deut. 6.5 and Lev. 19.18 in Jewish literature. Of course, that claim is reliable only if one presumes to have found a Jewish *Vorlage* earlier than our second-century CE Christian text.

Another interesting feature in the parenesis appears in 6.1-2a; 6.8-10.

Dan encourages flight to God and 'the angel who intercedes for you', a reference thought by some to reflect a 'primitive Christian angel-christology' (Hollander and de Jonge 1985: 291).

Dan's complex prognostications in 5.4-13; 6.2b-7 nurture the speculation regarding a pre-Christian form of the *Testaments* (e.g. Becker 1970; Charles 1908b; Hultgård 1977; Ulrichsen 1991). The references to the sins of the tribes of Levi and Judah under the influence of Dan's descendants are especially important in this respect (5.6-7). Some say that the text relates the sins of the two tribes to deeds of the late Hasmoneans (Charles 1908b: 128). Likewise, the reference in 5.10-13 to an eschatological new Jerusalem inaugurated by the saviour encourages speculation regarding supposedly related Hasmonean acts. But for all of this, the Christian elements in both passages are too well integrated to permit profitable conjecture regarding their pre-Christian form (of which there probably was one; see the acknowledgment of de Jonge 1953: 91-94; 1960: 225-26). That leaves us to comment on the present text (de Jonge 1986a: 207-209).

Testament of Dan 5.4-9 incorporates two L.J. passages (5.4, 6-7) into the framework of an S.E.R. text. *Testament of Dan* 5.4-7 gives the 'Sin' element, the 'Exile' portion appears in 5.8, and 5.9 narrates the tribe's 'Return'. In the first L.J. passage Dan tells his children that they will sin by opposing Levi and Judah, but the angel of the Lord will protect them from harm (5.4). The descendants' second sin will be idolatry (5.5; see above on the tribe's biblical reputation). Worse, they will take Satan as their prince (a claim similar to, but not the same as the Christian tradition that Dan's is the tribe of the Antichrist [Charles 1908b: 128-29; Hollander and de Jonge 1985: 287]). Under his deceitful influence they will use obedience to Levi and Judah to lead the priesthood and kingship into iniquity (5.6-7; for the sins of the kings and priests, see Ezek. 19.3, 6; 22.25; 44.10, 12). Exile will follow (5.8), but because of their repentance God will bring them back to God's sanctuary.

Several things in the following L.J. passage arouse interest. Elaborating on the 'R.' element in the preceding S.E.R. passage (5.9; cf. *T. Jud.* 24.1; *T. Zeb.* 9.8), Dan says that after the return, God will raise up a saviour from 'the tribe of Judah and Levi' who will successfully 'make war against Beliar' and bring humanity to obedience. To the obedient God will give eternal peace (5.10-11). The reversal of the typical order between Levi and Judah is intriguing, but unexplained. The use of the singular 'tribe' in relationship to Judah and Levi underscores the absence of dual messianism in the *Testaments* (so Nickelsburg and Stone 1983: 171). And the explicitly apocalyptic nature of this prediction—settling the conflict between heavenly and evil angels requires the intervention of

God's saviour—sets it apart from most of the other future predictions in the *Testaments* (Collins 1987: 91). The concluding declamation on the edenic nature of the new Jerusalem (5.12-13; cf. *T. Levi* 18.10) supports the apocalyptic understanding of the passage (Becker 1974: 96; Charles 1908b: 131, for parallel descriptions of the eschatological kingdom).

The remaining predictive text, 6.1-7, is also apocalyptic in nature. It reports on the battle between Satan and the mediating angel of God, and on God's decisive intervention. Satan works diligently to lead Israel astray since his power will end when they believe (6.3-4). But although the angel of peace (=God's angel) keeps the people from the worst sins and prevents their fall to Satan (6.2b, 5), the people still behave unlawfully and the Lord takes refuge from them among the 'Gentiles who do his will' with the result that his name is 'Saviour' among Jews and Gentiles (6.6-7; cf. Mal. 1.11, 14).

In another unusual structural feature, Dan offers final words of encouragement to his children (6.8-9) before ending with the standard conclusion (7.1-2; but see the late Christian gloss in 7.3). He says that they should avoid anger and lying, and love truth and long-suffering, especially since the 'saviour of the Gentiles' has those qualities, teaches the law through his deeds, and will come to those in Israel like him (cf. *T. Zeb.* 8.2-3; 9.7-8, where the same relationship between virtue, Israel and the messiah appears; cf. also *T. Levi* 16.3 for the notion of the messiah as the renewer of the law). Dan urges his tribe to leave all unrighteousness behind, and to cling to God's law so that they will be saved (6.10).

Dan's address affirms the *Testaments*' argument in several ways. The exhortation against anger implicitly equates Dan's instructions with popular Graeco-Roman views on the topic. Then Dan promises a messiah from the tribe(s) of Levi and Judah whose deeds will teach the law by confirming the importance of leading a life in conformity with Dan's exhortation. And finally Dan claims that belief in this saviour earns salvation, even after the tribe has rejected him once, and especially when faith is expressed by carrying out God's law as it appears in Dan's instructions and in the double commandment. In short, the testament promises to readers that if they behave as Dan and God propose—a way of life that happens also to be deemed honourable by the dominant Graeco-Roman culture—they will heed their ancestor's advice and receive salvation from the Christian messiah.

Testament of Naphtali

The *Testament of Naphtali*, on 'natural goodness', differs structurally from the other testaments. After the introduction (1.1-3) little follows in the typical order. Naphtali recollects events that, apart from one verse (2.1), have nothing to do with his own life history beyond his birth (1.4-11). He follows that with exhortation (2.2–3.5), an S.E.R. passage (4.1-5), two visions and Jacob's explanation of them (5.1–7.4), an L.J. passage (8.1-3), more exhortation (8.4-10), and the standard testamentary conclusion (9.1-3). Nevertheless, this testament, more than any other, makes absolutely transparent the coherence of God's wishes, expressed in the patriarchs' instructions and the double commandment, with Graeco-Roman standards of good conduct.

The testament's curious structure no doubt results from the authors' typical use of every available source (de Jonge 1953: 52-60; see also how the various theories regarding compositional history explain the testament's unusual shape; Becker 1970: 214-28; Charles 1908b: 135-48; Hultgård 1982: 128-35; Ulrichsen 1991: 145-61). Although it is surely not the very source used by the authors of the *Testaments*, 4QT(estament) N(aphtali) 1.2-5 parallels *T. Naph.* 1.9-12 (Bilhah's birth and genealogy; see DJD 22: 73-82). The scroll probably reflects a textual tradition which the *Testaments'* authors knew and used. Meanwhile, Naphtali's dreams in 5.1–7.4 and his description of the human body in 2.8 repeat material known from Hebrew *T. Naph.* 2–6; 10.5-7. Korteweg (1975) has demonstrated convincingly that the Greek testament loosely revised the Hebrew tradition (see discussion below; for more on 4Q215 and Hebrew *Testament of Naphtali*, see Chapter 1).

There is only a very slim biblical basis for Naphtali's biographical recollections. The explanation of Naphtali's name (1.6) develops elements of Gen. 30.3, 4, 8. And Naphtali's claim to be deer-like in his fleetness of foot (2.1) develops from a synoptic reading of Gen. 49.21 LXX and 2 Sam. 2.18. But Naphtali's recollection of Rachel's love for him, his 'tender appearance' in childhood, and Rachel's wish for a son just like Naphtali, fulfilled in Joseph (1.7-8), have no precedent in the Bible. There are, however, nonbiblical traditions that favourably associate Naphtali with Joseph. For example, in *Jos. Asen.* 25.5-7 (Burchard 1985) Naphtali and Asher resist Dan and Gad's plan to assist Pharaoh's son in his attack against Aseneth. In *Targ. Ps.-J.* Gen. 49.21 (Maher) Naphtali brings to Jacob the good news that Joseph lives (cf. 7.1-4). As for the genealogy of Bilhah in 1.9-12, it is only loosely connected with a number of biblical references (see the notes in Hollander and de Jonge 1985: 299-300).

The two separate hortatory units on 'natural goodness' (2.2–3.5; 8.4-10) epitomize the *Testaments'* ethics. The first unit integrates Graeco-Roman standards of conduct and notions of order in creation with Jewish and Christian norms (see the notes in Hollander and de Jonge 1985: 303-8; *pace* Becker 1974: 100). Naphtali begins by saying that God creates all things in coherence with their capacity and being, and that God knows how each thing will go, whether to the good or to the bad (2.2-5). Likewise, the human being exists and produces as he is possessed, whether by the law of God or the law of Beliar (2.6). One expresses a choice for one law or the other by one's response to the natural order that God has established in creation (2.7-9). Observing these facts, Naphtali urges his children to be thoughtful in their actions and to 'hold fast to the will of God' (3.1) as the sun, moon and stars do, and the Gentiles, Sodom and the Watchers did not (3.2-5; on the appearance of the Watchers, see Hollander and de Jonge 1985: 309-10; Williams 1980: 74-76; cf. *T. Reub.* 5.5-7).

After the predictive passages in 4.1–8.3 Naphtali again takes up the theme of natural goodness and God's order (8.4-10). In this passage he clearly integrates his exhortation to observe God's order and natural goodness with keeping the double commandment. He beseeches his children to 'work good' (which by now means living by the natural order made clear in 2.2–3.5) so that God will be glorified among the Gentiles, men and angels will cleave to them, Beliar will flee from them, beasts will fear them, and the Lord will love them; doing evil, says Naphtali, brings the opposite results (8.4-6). The way to make sure one achieves this is by keeping the commandments of the Lord, which themselves reflect the ordered nature of God's creation (8.7). In a play on Eccl. 3.1-11, Naphtali then points out that there is a time for intercourse with one's wife (love of one's neighbour) and a time for prayer (love of God); if these things are done out of their order (the 'order' of marital intercourse having been made clear in the speeches of Reuben, Judah and Issachar) they 'bring sin' (8.8-9). So, concludes Naphtali, pay attention to the order of God's 'commandments and the laws of all human activity so that the Lord will love you' (8.10).

Stepping back from the details of his parenesis, it is easy to see that Naphtali's lengthy argument boils down to several propositions. First, 'doing what is good' fulfils God's twofold commandment and pleases God (8.4-10). Second, one does good by doing the right thing at the right time, for the right people, for the right reasons, and with the right resources (2.6, 9-10; 3.1-5; 8.4-6). And three, what is right was determined in the first place by God (2.2-8). Thus Naphtali argues that God made it possible for the believer to please God simply by living reasonably, that is, according to natural goodness. Naphtali's satisfaction with his role as the family messenger, to which he was suited by the way God created him, proves the veracity of this analysis (2.1).

By contrast, Naphtali's predictions of his tribe's future indicate Israel's reluctance to please God. Naphtali's double S.E.R. passage comes to him by way of the now familiar 'holy writing of Enoch'. It reveals that Naphtali's descendants will fail to live according to natural goodness. Instead they will do as the Gentiles and Sodom (4.1; cf. 3.3, 4), go into captivity (4.2), and repent and be restored by God to the land (4.3). But they will sin again through (undefined) impiety (4.4), be scattered, and be restored by the compassion of the coming Lord, God's saviour (4.5).

Probably because Naphtali's tribe is said to depend on the mercy of God in the coming saviour from the tribes of Levi and Judah, the authors of the *Testaments* included a redacted form of Naphtali's two visions from the Hebrew *Testament of Naphtali* before the L.J. passage in 8.1-3 (Korteweg 1975; de Jonge 1953: 52-60). They show Levi's and Judah's elevated status. In the first vision (5.1-8) Levi and Judah act in concert to seize the sun and the moon (and Joseph rides a bull into the heavens). By contrast, Hebrew *T. Naph.* 2–3 says nothing of cooperation between Levi and Judah and portrays Joseph as their antagonist (on the list of peoples in 5.8 and its possible significance for dating the *Testaments*, see Becker 1974: 25-26, 103; Charles 1908b: 143-44; Hengel 1974: 182; contrast, however, Hollander and de Jonge 1985: 312). The second vision (6.1-10) also highlights the importance of Levi and Judah in providing hope for Israel's future. It recounts a shipwreck involving Jacob and his sons. Levi and Judah share a piece of flotsam (while Joseph 'fled away in a little boat' [6.6]). Levi's intercessory prayer delivers the brothers and reunites them with their father on the seashore (6.8-10). Again, by contrast the Hebrew account (*T. Naph.* 4–6 [MT]) blames the wreck on Levi, Judah and Joseph, and credits Jacob with reuniting the family on the shore. Finally, when Naphtali related these visions to Jacob, his father said they were predictions of the future (7.1; and in an aside [7.2-4] the two comment on the likelihood that Joseph still lives in light of his appearance in Naphtali's visions). So it is that Naphtali follows this biographical recollection with the L.J. admonition to 'unite with Levi and Judah' because Israel's saviour (and the one who gathers the righteous from the Gentiles) will come through Judah (8.1-3; note that here the saviour comes through Judah alone; on this see, e.g., Charles 1908b: 146; on the clause dealing with the righteous Gentiles and its Jewish or Christian origin, see Becker 1970: 227; 1974: 104; Beasley-Murray 1947: 3-4, 8; Hultgård 1977: 76; Ulrichsen 1991: 160). After all, in the first vision Levi and Judah demonstrated their control over nature and the light of the heavenly luminaries, and in the second Levi especially rescued Jacob's sons (compare Hilgert 1986, who suggests that the shipwreck is a symbol of the events of 132–35 CE, and the picture of a reunited family of Jacob on the seashore is the Christian authors' expression of hope that Israel will come to faith in the messiah and be restored).

Clearly this testament's most significant contribution to the *Testaments'* argument regarding Israel's salvation lies in its parenesis. Naphtali's speech assigns God the responsibility for having established the natural goodness of order in creation. In turn Naphtali says that proper conduct is merely a matter of living according to that order. In this way Naphtali's speech, more clearly than any other, coalesces Graeco-Roman standards of reasonable conduct with the teaching of the patriarch and of God's saviour. And Naphtali makes it equally clear that even if Israel misunderstands his instructions and lives against natural goodness and God's law, God will still send a saviour to offer yet another avenue to salvation.

Testament of Gad

Gad's speech on anger returns to the theme explored already in Dan's address (but Dan laboured under θυμός, while Gad's burden was μισός). The testament generally adheres to the standard structure. There is the usual introduction and conclusion (1.1-2; 8.3-5), biography (1.2–2.5), parenesis (3.1–7.7) and forecast of the future (8.1-2). His speech only departs from the pattern by providing a snippet of biographical testimony in the middle of the parenesis (5.9-11; see Becker 1974: 108, for the inevitable, though unnecessary, speculation that this departure reflects redactional activity)

In his autobiographical comments Gad first relates that he was valorous in his service as a shepherd, taking on any carnivorous beast that threatened the flock and killing it in the most dramatic fashion (1.2-3). At first this observation seems to be unrelated to the rest of Gad's speech, much less to anything else we know of Gad or Gadites. In fact, the only biblical event remotely associated with such a story is that of David in 1 Sam. 17.34-35 (cf. *T. Jud.* 2.2-7). But in fact, Gad's self-aggrandizing account plays a critical role in the rest of his personal story. It provides the necessary background for understanding the 'bad report' Joseph gave to Jacob about the sons of Zilpah and Bilhah (Gen. 37.2), and thus, in turn, for Gad's anger at Joseph. For so it seems, Joseph, too delicate to last long in the fields with his brothers and the flocks (1.4), returned to his father's house with heat-stroke. Upon arriving he reported to Jacob that 'the sons of Zilpah and Bilhah are slaying the best of the flock and are eating them' (1.6; paralleled only in part in *Targ. Ps.-J.* Gen. 37.2 [the sons eat the flesh of living livestock; Clarke]). Gad tells his children, however, that what Joseph saw was a demonstration of his intrepidity as a shepherd. One day a bear mauled a lamb. Catching the bear in the act Gad summarily dismantled it and then reluctantly euthanized the mortally wounded sheep. It was the latter action that Joseph witnessed. Thus Gad's murderous anger (1.9; 2.1-2, 4), the focus of the testament, was generated by Joseph's misapprehension of Gad's action as a valorous shepherd and by his rash report to his father on that conduct (Gen. 37.2). We return to the significance of this synoptic reading of Gen. 37.2 and 1 Sam. 17.34-35 in Chapter 3 below.

The rest of the biographical material exhibits two other interesting characteristics. Only here in the *Testaments* does Joseph come in for any kind of criticism. Gad describes him as 'delicate' (1.4), a none too laudatory comment when masculinity and its prowess were highly regarded. In addition, Joseph's story for Jacob of his brothers' treachery was just that—a story with no basis in fact (1.6). By contrast, Joseph's elevated role still manages to make an appearance here as well: as much as Gad hated Joseph and wanted to kill him, he could not because God, protecting once more the beloved Joseph, delivered him from harm.

Another intriguing element of Gad's autobiographical report comes in his report that he and Judah took 30 pieces of gold for Joseph (2.3). The Bible, meanwhile, records a sale price of only 20 pieces (Gen. 37.28 LXX). Hollander and de Jonge (1985: 323) explain this as testimony to the brothers' greed; after all, they do pocket the difference between their fee and the biblical sum. Others view this as a Christian comment related to Judas' price for Jesus; thus the reference would add to a list of 'Joseph-as-type-of-Jesus' passages (Charles 1908b: 151; de Jonge 1953: 101; cf. *T. Zeb.* 3.3; 4.4). Still others point out that the 30 pieces recall Exod. 21.32; Zech. 11.12-13 (Becker 1970: 338), and may have nothing to do with Christian connections between Joseph and Jesus.

The first parenesis unit (3.1–5.2), a discourse on the evil effects of hatred, mixes once again the insights of the classical moralists and Graeco-Roman philosophy with Jewish and Christian motifs (see the notes in Hollander and de Jonge 1985: 326-28). Indeed, the structuring of 3.1-3 followed by 4.1–5.2, though barely noticeable, makes the first part resemble a classical moralist's discourse and the second reflect a more theologically-grounded exposition on the topic of anger. 3.1-3 focuses on the effects of hatred, while 4.1–5.2 supports the claim that hatred allies itself with Satan, and love is in league with God.

Not surprisingly, much of this parenesis repeats themes encountered already in Simeon's and Dan's speeches (cf. especially the reference to hatred and envy together in 4.5 and in *T. Sim.* 3.3). But at its heart, this speech against anger and jealousy is different from the two earlier addresses; it reflects the *Testaments'* gradually intensified connection between the double commandment and worthy conduct, for *T. Gad* 4.2-4 argues that hatred violates the double commandment. First Gad says that hate turns a deaf ear to the commandment to love one's neighbour and it spawns sin against God (4.2). To illustrate this, Gad describes a hater's desire to punish sinners in extreme ways, and a hateful servant's murderous intentions for his master (4.3-4). The rush to capital punishment (4.3) constitutes hate's violation of the commandment to love one's neighbour (4.2a); the servant's homicidal rage against the master (4.4) symbolizes the violation of the requirement to love the Lord (4.2b).

An allusion to Jesus is also apparent within the first section of parenesis. In 4.6 Gad says that while hate wants to kill all things and has no compassion even for those who are 'only a little sinful' (a reference to Joseph and his 'bad report' to Jacob?), love seeks life, even going so far as to restore it where it has been extinguished and to work to save the condemned (cf. 1.6; 2.2; see the additional notes in Hollander and de Jonge 1985: 327, indicating an even deeper literary pool for the notion of God loving by giving life). The reference to Jesus as a miracle worker and redeemer of the lost is transparent.

In 5.3-11 Gad offers an excursus between the first parenesis on hatred (3.1–5.2) and the second on love (6.1–7.7). He explains that through repentance he discovered that righteousness and humility put hatred to death, for the righteous and humble man knows that God sees all and therefore fears giving offence to the Most High. Two aspects of this excursus stand out. First, 5.6-8 combines Jewish, Christian and Hellenistic conversion language in a notable fashion. For instance, in 5.7 Gad says that repentance of hatred leads to human enlightenment, a notion that echoes the Stoic idea that discipline of the spirit frees the person from vices. Yet, in a Jewish-Christian touch, 5.8 adds that whatever the soul does not learn from the experience of others, the act of repentance—return to God—imparts. Also, 5.9-11 reveals the *Testaments'* approach to determining punishments for vice: one is afflicted in that part of the body that offends (cf. *T. Reub.* 1.7; on 'exegetical misdirection' in *T. Sim.* 2.12-13, see Chapter 3).

The second hortatory segment addresses love as the counterpoint to hatred. The focus of the speech is on how love responds to slanderous and unusually prosperous neighbours (6.1–7.7). Gad implies that he speaks on these topics from experience (6.2), but few recognize that the experience of which he speaks is with Joseph! Joseph defamed Gad with his inaccurate report (1.6), and surely Jacob's greater love for Joseph (1.5), Joseph's prophecy of his greater glory vis-à-vis his brothers (2.2), and his material success in Egypt (cf. 3.3; 4.5) all galled Gad. Having suffered the consequences of failing in his response to Joseph's slander and greater prosperity, Gad counsels his children to act in love. On behalf of the liar they should exercise mercy borne of Graeco-Roman style prudence and the Jewish-Christian inclination to forgive (6.3-7; see the references in Hollander and de Jonge 1985: 333-34). And with respect to the justly or unjustly wealthy, they should understand, as the people of Israel, that God's desire will be done for them just as it is for the prosperous; moreover, should God chose poverty for them, they should be glad, since indigence makes a man rich by freeing 'him from pain and sorrow which accompany riches' (a Stoic–Cynic notion; Hollander and de Jonge 1985: 335 [with citations to Plutarch and Epictetus on poverty's benefits]).

The testament closes with a J.L. passage, remarkable only for its reversal of the usual order in speaking of Judah first. Its perfunctory nature betrays the testament's general lack of interest in future prediction. Almost more is said of Israel's future in the allusion to Jesus in 4.6 (see above).

Gad's speech, then, extends and reinforces the *Testaments*' argument mostly by intensifying the connections between Graeco-Roman standards of good conduct, the character of the saviour messiah (see 4.6), and the keeping of the double commandment. Following Gad's advice leads naturally to a life lived well in the Graeco-Roman world, but it would also be a life quite pleasing in God's sight.

Testament of Asher

Asher's testament concerns obeying God's commandments with a 'single face'. It contains virtually no biography, referring only to Asher having always done what was right (5.4). Asher's predictions of the future consist of a double S.E.R. passage in 7.1-7. Otherwise the speech gives exhortation with accompanying explanation and examples (1.3–6.6). Its introduction and conclusion are unremarkable. But what does set the testament apart is its clear-cut articulation of the *Testaments*' otherwise subtle 'decision theology'.

The testament's theme requires extra attention. Asher argues that God creates everything in twos, each thing having its opposite (1.4). By analogy there are two ways of being, good and evil, and there are two corresponding dispositions in the human heart (1.5). While Asher's speech seems to propose a two-ways theology (cf. 1QS 3.13–4.26 [Vermes]; *Barnabas* 18–20; *Shepherd of Hermas, Mandates* VI.1-2 [Lake]), almost all commentators speak against that conclusion, and rightly so (e.g., Becker 1970: 369; Collins 1983: 160-61; Hollander and de Jonge 1985: 339). It is true that Asher speaks of 'two dispositions' as though there are two διαβούλιοι, 'inclinations', in the human heart. However, the testament proves that there is but one διαβούλιον that is shaped for good or for bad by human choice. Moreover, the testament lacks ethical and cosmic dualism, hallmarks of the two-ways theology. Only when it introduces the two spirits, one evil (6.5; cf. 1.8, 9; 3.2; 6.2; Beliar [and his minions]), and the other an angel of peace (6.6), does the testament come close to this sort of dualism. But even here the authors only seem to know a dualistic angelology that they adapt for their own use (for this argument and references see Hollander and de Jonge 1985: 337, 357). While the evil spirit and God's angel influence a person's choices (as they do throughout the *Testaments*), in the end the individual's fate is still under his or her own control. After all, in 6.4-6, a key passage for understanding the testament's angelology, the two spirits are simply there waiting at death to torment or comfort the humans who cast their lot with them in life. Furthermore, 3.2 goes so far as to say that good human deeds can even destroy the devil.

This testament's one-verse biography (5.4) relies on no recognizable scripture. However, other parts of the testament occasionally exhibit direct reliance on the Bible. Most conspicuously, Asher depends on Lev. 11.2b-8 and Deut. 14.3-20 regarding the impurity of hares and pigs to describe the 'two-faced man' (διπρόσωπος) who has chosen evil as a way of being (2.9). Just as the hare and the pig appear outwardly to be clean, but are intrinsically impure, so also a man may appear to do good, but does so out of evil and is thus wholly evil (note the reference to 'heavenly tablets' as the medium by which Asher knows of a hare's and pig's impurity; the laws of purity had not yet been given). Likewise, in 4.5 Asher refers to the stag and the hind, pure animals according to Deut. 14.5, to describe the man who does what appears to be evil, but does so out of good motives and so is wholly good.

Another direct reference to Scripture appears in 7.1. Asher tells his children that those who choose righteousness in life will die peacefully for they will recognize the angel of peace greeting them at their death. As for the wicked, they will be in anguish at the moment of their passing, for they will see an evil spirit. In light of these observations, Asher slips in a loosely-related allusion to Gen. 19, telling his children not to be 'as Sodom, that did not know the angels of the Lord'.

A number of other items within the two major parts of this testament merit attention. Reflecting the evermore manifest emphasis on the double commandment, the structure of 2.1–4.5 places an exhortation to keep the two commands at the centre of its discourse about the 'two-faced' nature of human beings. *T. Ash.* 2.1-10 uses the language of classical moralists to describe the behaviour and intentions of the man who has chosen an evil disposition (so Asher's claim that the man with a wicked disposition will even die for a fellow evil-doer [2.3] echoes the 'Hellenistic' friendship ethic; cf. Plutarch, *Moralia* 244D [Babbitt *et al.*]; Epictetus, *Discourses* II.7.3 [Oldfather]). But then 3.1-2 echoes the double commandment, with the language, 'cleave to goodness, for God rests upon it and men desire it' (3.1); 3.2 adds that by doing so you 'destroy the devil with your good actions' (cf. *T. Iss.* 7.7; *T. Dan* 5.1-2; *T. Naph.* 8.4; *T. Benj.* 5.2, where keeping the commandments or doing good drives Beliar away). Then 4.1-5 mirrors 2.1-10, giving examples of men who do what appear to be evil deeds for good reasons, and who therefore possess a good inclination. But unlike 2.1-10, this passage uses scriptural rhetoric to make its point (Hollander and de Jonge 1985: 352, cite the use in 4.4 of Ps. 34.12 [LXX 33.13], a man with a good disposition will not wait to see a good day if it must be spent with evil-doers). Thus the double commandment stands at the heart of a patriarch's exhortation once more, and in this case its use even seems to transform the tone of the patriarch's Hellenistic rhetoric so that it becomes biblical in tenor.

Two items of interest turn up in the double S.E.R. passage (7.1-7). In the first presentation of the pattern (7.1-3) Asher describes Israel's mistakes under kings and their consequent exile (7.1-2). But then he leaps forward in time to describe God's visitation to Israel 'as a man, eating and drinking with men and in silence breaking the head of the dragon through water' (7.3b). The reference to Jesus is unmistakable, but in yet another direct use of Scripture Asher quotes and adjusts Ps. 74 [LXX 73].13-14; in the Psalm the dragon's head is broken *in* water, while here the preposition becomes διά, 'through', undoubtedly to signify the water of baptism (cf. *T. Levi* 16.5). Most imagine that the reference is to baptism in general, yet Ps. 74 [LXX 73].12-15 announces *God* coming into the waters to liberate the oppressed; by analogy it is thus not too far-fetched to imagine that *T. Ash.* 7.3 recalls Jesus' own baptism.

The second item of interest in 7.1-7 is the *Testaments'* only explicit indication that faith in Jesus alone suffices to please God. Asher predicts his descendants' disobedience toward the coming Lord and their resulting exile (7.5-6). Then he says that he looks forward to the day when the Lord will gather the tribe 'in faith through hope on his [God's] compassion (εὐσπλαγχνία), for the sake of Abraham and Isaac and Jacob' (7.7). Inasmuch as *T. Zeb.* 8.2 calls Jesus God's compassion (σπλάγχνον), the implication here is clear: lawkeeping, at least in this instance, is not necessary for salvation; faith in God's compassion, Jesus, suffices.

Asher's speech affirms the *Testaments'* argument by making clear once more the congruence between keeping God's double commandment and Hellenistic moral standards. But it also advances the thesis by making clearer than ever before in the *Testaments* that they promote a 'decision theology'. One decides for God either by doing what is pleasing to God through adherence to the teaching of the patriarchs, or by embracing the saviour from God (7.7).

Testament of Joseph

This testament is the second longest. Because of its size, its diverse sources, and its dedication to one of the central figures in the *Testaments*, it has garnered ample attention (see, among others, Braun 1938; Hilgert 1985; H.W. Hollander 1981; Niehoff 1992; and the essays by Pervo, Harrelson, Hollander, M. de Jonge and Korteweg, Harrington, and Smith in Nickelsburg 1975). Mostly it addresses Joseph's endurance as the key to his salvation/exaltation. His chastity toward Potiphar's wife and his honourable treatment for his brothers give concrete expression to his endurance. Much of the testament's size comes from its extended biography, which in turn seems aimed at providing ample opportunity to illustrate Joseph's endurance. After the typical opening passage (1.1-2) and an introductory psalm of thanksgiving that recalls God's favour for him (1.3–2.7), Joseph recounts his chastity and endurance in dealing with Potiphar's wife (3.1–9.5) and exhorts his children to a similar commitment to purity, humility and endurance (10.1-4). Then he introduces the second story (10.5–11.1) and tells how the Egyptian and his wife came to possess him and how he hid his status from all concerned to save his brothers' reputations (11.2–16.6). Next Joseph exhorts his children to love each other and to minimize their neighbours' flaws (17.1–18.4). Finally Joseph recounts his vision of Israel's future dispersal and Jesus' deliverance of them (19.1-4) and he urges his children to heed Levi and Judah since their deliverer will come from them (19.6-7). The testament's conclusion (20.1-6) is longer than usual. It provides instructions regarding the removal of Joseph's bones from Egypt to Canaan at the exodus and the burial of Zilpah near Bilhah and Rachel, and it tells of mourning among Israelites and Egyptians at Joseph's death.

As noted, the testament's theme is how endurance, expressed in Joseph's chastity and concern for his brothers, leads to salvation and exaltation. So while the material used to tell his story may be disparate in nature, the biography and parenesis work together to make a single point (H.W. Hollander 1981: 48; note especially how Hollander uses this observation against those who would posit a lengthy compositional history; e.g., Becker 1970: 228-43; Charles 1908b: 172-97; Ulrichsen

1991: 110-18). However a closer look suggests that the unity of the testament runs even deeper than that. The speech is an elaboration on Joseph's comment to his brothers that while they meant to do him evil, God meant it all for good (Gen. 50.20): through testing, Joseph proves the human capacity to keep God's double commandment. The first story shows that Joseph, when confronted with temptation and threat, returned time and again to God in prayer, fasting, charity and intercession for others. Rather than give in to temptation, Joseph chose to love God. The second story, meanwhile, proves Joseph's fulfilment of the second central commandment, to love one's neighbour. At great cost to himself he saves his brothers' reputations. The good, then, that came of Joseph's suffering was the test of his ability to keep the two commandments and his exaltation and salvation for having met the challenge. Thus the testament proves how Joseph deserves his reputation as a model of ethical conduct in the *Testaments*. He epitomizes the proper posture vis-à-vis God. Not to be forgotten is the fact that the virtue promoted in this testament is a core value of the Cynic–Stoic ethic. Endurance, ὑπομονή/μακροθυμία, is the key to controlling the passions and avoiding the other vices addressed in the *Testaments*. So Joseph is also the model Graeco-Roman citizen.

Joseph begins making this argument in an individual thanksgiving (1.3–2.7) that clearly echoes Gen. 50.20. By repeating the equivalent of the refrain, 'I was afflicted, but God delivered me', this late individual thanksgiving (cf. Dan. 2.20-23; Sir. 51.1-12; see Ps. 18 [LXX 17].18; 116 [LXX 114].6; Jon. 2.2 for earlier forms; H.W. Hollander 1981: 31-33; Hollander and de Jonge 1985: 367) implicitly raises the question that the rest of the testament answers. What was God's purpose in permitting this to happen? How could God have made good come from these circumstances?

The first story begins to answer the question. It builds from Gen. 39.6b-18 and the abundant resources of Hellenistic romances ten 'tests' of Joseph's endurance and chastity (see especially the Phaedra tradition; secondary discussions include Braun 1938; Hollander and de Jonge 1985: 372-73; de Jonge 1953: 102-106; Pervo 1975; Thomas 1969), and a portrait of Joseph as a man of piety in the face of temptation. As a servant in Photimar's house (on the name see 2.1 and the discussion in Hollander and de Jonge 1985: 374) Joseph is 'invited' ten times over to have intercourse with his master's wife (3.1–9.5). The eighth invitation (8.2-5) reproduces the basic elements of Gen. 39.6b-18. Of the remaining nine, some stand out in particular for their similarity with Hellenistic romances; see, for instance, the woman's offer to murder her husband and Joseph's threat to reveal her plan to Photimar (5.1-4); the woman's use of a magic potion either to lull Joseph into submission or kill him (6.1-9); and the woman's threat to suicide (7.1–8.1; on all of these, see Braun 1938; Hollander and de Jonge 1985: 372-73; Pervo 1975). As for Joseph's piety—that is to say, his keeping of the commandment to love God above all else—he gives himself repeatedly to prayer, fasting, charity, pleas for deliverance and intercession for the woman (3.3-6, 10; 4.3, 8; 5.2; 6.3, 6-8; 7.4b-5, 8.1b; note that this orientation toward God is what links Joseph's abstinence to Rachel in *T. Iss.* 1.3–2.5). The end result, of course, is Joseph's ironic deliverance from temptation through imprisonment, for which he gives thanks and praise to God, exhibiting once more his orientation to the Divine and his adherence to the commandment to love God (8.4–9.5). This part of the testament concludes with Joseph's exhortation to his children to act as he did when they are confronted with tribulation (10.1-4).

All agree that the second story in 10.5–18.4 uses different sources from those utilized in 2.1–10.4. A number of things point to this conclusion. First, the second story narrates events that would have taken place before the first story. Second, in the second story the woman is called 'the Memphian woman' (12.1; 14.1, 5; 16.1) and her husband's name changes to 'Petephres' (12.1; 13.1, 4; 15.6; cf. 2.1). And, third, the narrative treats the woman's appearance in 12.1 as though it were for the first time (Hollander and de Jonge 1985: 393).

The second story provides the proof that keeping God's second commandment, to love one's brother, also leads to exaltation and deliverance. Moreover, Joseph links the keeping of the first commandment to the second by introducing the story with a speech that says fear of God leads to honour and respect for the other (10.5–11.1). He then supports that claim with the story of his sale to the Ishmaelites and subsequent purchase by the 'Memphian woman' (11.2–16.6). At the heart of the tale is Joseph's lie every time the Ishmaelites or Petephres ask him whether he was free-born; to protect his brothers' honour and reputation he tells his owners that he is a slave (11.3; 13.6-8; 14.2; 15.3; see also 10.6; 17.1, and note the connection to Asher's speech on the man with the good disposition who does what only *appears* to be evil, but, borne of a good spirit, works good [*T. Ash.* 4.1-5]). Just for good measure, the author tells us that when the eunuch cheats the Memphian woman of twenty pieces of gold as her agent in purchasing Joseph from the Ishmaelites, Joseph keeps his silence to save the eunuch (16.4-6; note that on the basis of the term used for the pieces of gold ['minae'] Bickerman 1950: 256-59, posits an early second century BCE date for the *Testaments*!). In both cases Joseph doggedly keeps God's commandment to love one's neighbour.

Finally, drawing on the story of his concern for his brothers, Joseph tells his children in the following parenesis (17.1–18.4) that he was exalted and rewarded with beauty and marriage to a daughter of his masters (18.3-4; de Jonge 1953: 109-10, discusses and cites the two Jewish traditions preserved here; compare *Joseph and Aseneth*); seeing those rewards, they should emulate him in this regard. And with that Joseph has made his argument as to how God achieved good through his suffering (cf. Gen. 50.20).

Joseph's future predictions are relatively unremarkable, although the longer, apocalyptic variant in the Armenian version naturally generates considerable interest among those who focus attention on the *Testaments'* compositional history and place some trust in the Armenian version's differences as indicators of earlier forms of the work (Becker 1970: 243; Charles 1908b: 191-95; Hultgård 1977: 213-26; Ulrichsen 1991: 119). But since the Leiden school proved the Armenian to be an unreliable witness it seems best to read the text as it appears in the Greek manuscripts. In an allusion to Jesus, Joseph reports a vision in which the twelve tribes, symbolized by deer, are attacked and dispersed, but are delivered by a combative lamb, born of a virgin of Judah (19.1-5). Then Joseph gives an L.J. passage, urging his children to heed the tribes of Levi and Judah for the lamb will come from them and establish a kingdom that will replace Joseph's (19.6-7).

On the whole, then, Joseph's testament impressively sustains the *Testaments'* claim that Graeco-Roman standards of conduct are compatible with the patriarchs' instructions, the double commandment of God, and the teaching and ministry of Jesus. All that is left for the authors is to summarize their claims in the *Testament of Benjamin*.

Testament of Benjamin

Benjamin's testament is hardly his own. Instead Joseph dominates everything his younger brother says about the testament's topic, the 'good man', ὁ ἀγαθὸς ἀνήρ. Moreover, the speech clearly sets out to summarize the *Testaments'* larger argument about the relationships among ethics, eschatology and theology, echoing along the way virtually all of the other patriarchs' themes. As a result it is hardly surprising that Benjamin all but recedes from view in his own testament.

The speech exhibits a complex structure. After the usual introduction (1.1-2a) Benjamin gives condensed biographical details (1.2b–2.5). Then he gives parenesis that returns occasionally to details from Joseph's life as illustrative material (3.1–8.3). Future predictions also make an appearance in this section (3.8), but only in 9.1-5 and 10.6-11 does Benjamin offer full-blown predictions of the future. In 10.1-5 and 11.1-5 he offers the

Testaments' last commandments and announces the coming of the 'beloved of the Lord' from his own seed (Paul). The concluding passage is typical apart from a reference to the war between Egypt and the people of Canaan (12.1-4; cf. *T. Gad* 8.5).

Because especially the Armenian version of Benjamin's speech lacks much of the overtly 'Christian' material preserved in the Greek text (on the general phenomenon in the *Testaments*, see Conybeare 1893), the testament is used heavily by those who seek to establish a pre-Christian form of the *Testaments*. *Testament of Benjamin* 3.8 and 9–11 draw especially intense interest (Becker 1970: 48-57; 1974: 132-33, 135-37; Charles 1908b: 202, 209-217; de Jonge 1989b; Ulrichsen 1991: 136-44). But Stone's treatment of the Armenian version (1977) proves that the minuses probably have nothing to do with Jewish or Christian interests. Rather, they resulted from a slothful scribe's ever more frequent omission of portions of text as he worked his way through the *Testaments* (M. de Jonge 1975a).

Since Benjamin says so little of himself, there is equally scant use of Scripture to build his biography in the testament. *Testament of Benjamin* 1.6 relies on Gen. 35.18 (Benjamin's naming); 2.1 recalls Gen. 43.16, 29 (Benjamin's arrival in Egypt and Joseph's recognition of him); and 2.1-4 plays off of elements in Gen. 37.6b-18 (also compare 2.4 and 1 Kgs 13.24). Nevertheless, Scripture makes some obvious cameo appearances in the rest of the speech. The prediction of the lamb of God in 3.8 clearly takes up images from Isa. 52.13–53.12. The description of the man under Beliar's control as driven by envy in 7.3-5 uses the story of Cain (Gen. 4.1-16). And the description of Paul as a ravenous wolf, a distributor of food, and the beloved of God in 11.1-2 recalls Jacob's blessing for Benjamin in Gen. 49.27 and Moses' blessing for the tribe in Deut. 33.12.

As for the content of the testament, it is an exposition of the 'good man' who has a 'good mind' (3.1-2; ὁ ἀγαθὸς ἀνήρ/ἡ ἀγαθὴ διάνοια). Joseph serves throughout as the model of this sort of man. H.W. Hollander (1981: 65-92) and Hollander and de Jonge (1985: 413) have noted that the terms ὁ ἀγαθὸς ἀνήρ and ἡ ἀγαθὴ διάνοια are terms borrowed from the classical moralists (see Plutarch, *Moralia* 121F [Babbitt *et al.*]; Epictetus, *Discourses* II.3.1; III.24.50-51 [Oldfather]; see Hollander and de Jonge 1985: 413 for other citations). Nevertheless, the authors of the *Testaments* give the terms meaning that is coherent with concepts from Septuagintal wisdom literature, notions that were also popular among other Jewish and Christian writers around the turn of the era (see, for example, the description of the good man as righteous in Prov. 30.23 LXX; Sir. 29.14). When examined from an even broader perspective it is also clear that the author used adherence to the double commandment as the overarching explanation of how one achieves the status of a 'good man' (see 3.1-4). Consequently, as the *Testaments* have argued from the beginning, the patriarch's advice to his descendants is to live as the Graeco-Roman world would have them live, for in doing so they keep God's commandments, and prepare for the coming of God's saviour.

The testament's peculiar structure underscores its argument. It is no accident that the overture to the parenesis begins with direct exhortation (3.1), then urges the keeping of the two commandments (3.2-5), illustrates their keeping with an anecdote about Joseph (3.6-7), and concludes with anticipation of the saviour by using Joseph as a type of Jesus (3.8). This mirrors the outline of the rest of the parenesis and the future predictions. Beginning and closing with direct exhortation (4.1; 8.1-3), Benjamin's hortatory material describes the qualities of the good man twice over in 4.1–6.7 and those of the good man's opposite, the evil man, in 7.1-5. Along the way Benjamin uses Joseph to illustrate the nature of the good man, describes such a man's virtues in language typical of Hellenistic popular philosophy and of early Judaism and Christianity, and provides repeated hints of the double commandment. As usual, future predictions follow (9.1–11.5), at the centre of which stands the promised saviour.

The contents of the parenesis also confirm the view that sums up the *Testaments'* argument. Its portrait of the good man echoes virtually all of the positive and negative Greek, Jewish and Christian traits addressed by the other patriarchs (see the notes in Hollander and de Jonge 1985: 422-33). In using ἀνδρεῖος ('valiant' or 'manly') and σώφρων ('prudent') to describe two qualities of the good man (4.4), Benjamin holds up two of the central Hellenistic virtues and echoes with the first Judah's particular virtue. In the same verse the ascription of συμπάθεια, 'sympathy', to the good man recalls Zebulun's virtue. Holding one's peace and praying for the other when one is threatened or harmed (5.4-5) is Joseph's special gift. The good man's moderation in sexuality and possessions (6.2-3) calls to mind Judah and Reuben. Not letting triumph or tribulation move one (6.4) recalls Naphtali (*T. Naph.* 3.1). Benjamin's insistence that the good man is simple and has no double-mindedness about him (6.5-7) calls to mind Asher and Issachar. And the reference to envy and the troubles it brings in its train calls Simeon, Dan and Gad to mind. Not surprisingly, only Levi's speech is not obviously echoed in Benjamin's parenesis.

The nature of the future-oriented material also verifies the claim that Benjamin's speech is a grand conclusion to the larger work. The first passage, 9.1-5, preserves an S.E.R.+E. passage that culminates in the rejection of the saviour upon his arrival. This, along with renewed exhortation to keep the commandments (10.3-5), sets the stage for the resurrection passage that follows in 10.6-11. There Benjamin confirms that with the arrival of the saviour (for the second time) Enoch, Noah, Shem, Abraham, Isaac and Jacob will be raised, and in their turn each of the patriarchs will rise from the dead to worship 'the king of heaven, who appeared on earth in the form of a man of humility' (10.7). Then all will be raised, Gentile and Jew, who believed in the saviour and all who did not give their faith to him will be judged (10.8-10). So, says Benjamin, his children should prepare for the moment by 'walking in holiness before the Lord'. To conclude the future predictions, Benjamin predicts that Paul, God's missionary to the Gentiles from Benjamin's seed, will also 'supply the needs' of those from whom he came, the tribe of Benjamin, and of all of Israel (11.1-5).

Thus the *Testaments* end with a final speech from the youngest of Jacob's sons, a speech that confirms the message provided all along for Jewish and Christian recipients. Keeping the word of the patriarchs, obeying the double commandment, getting along in the Graeco-Roman world, and accepting and obeying God's saviour, Jesus, are all one and the same. Moreover, as especially the life of Joseph proves, all such endeavours are well within the capacity of any Jewish or Christian recipient of the patriarchs' sayings. And should there be any fear that past sins—committed either through omission with respect to the law, or the commission of acts against the saviour—might doom the people forever, Benjamin provides a response to that as well. Like the other patriarchs, he confirms that this saviour will come again to offer still one more chance for Israel to seize the fate that God offers.

Further Reading

The only recent commentary on the *Testaments of the Twelve Patriarchs* is Hollander and de Jonge (1985). In addition one does well to consult Becker (1974), although it amounts to little more than a translation of the text with text-critical notes and only a few content notes. Before these two, of course, there was the seminal work offered by Charles (1908b, 1913). Charles' comments, however, are always to be treated with care because they so thoroughly reflect his peculiar view of the *Testaments'* compositional and textual histories. One can also consult Kee (1983), although little comment is provided beyond a translation of the text.

In addition to these commentaries the reader should consult the more specialized studies of Becker (1970), Hultgård (1977, 1982), and Ulrichsen (1991). None of these qualifies as a commentary on the *Testaments*, and all of them are more interested in attending to composition-historical questions than they are inclined to address the meaning of the *Testaments* as they come to us. Nonetheless one can on occasion glean from them some insight into the character of the Christian work that survives.

Apart from the aforementioned books, all of the article-length studies written by M. de Jonge (listed in the Bibliography) are of signal importance in the studying the specifics of the *Testaments*. In addition we may look forward to James Kugel's commentary on the *Testaments* in the Hermeneia series.

3

EXEGESIS AND THEOLOGY IN THE
TESTAMENTS OF THE TWELVE PATRIARCHS

At least in part, the *Testaments* rely on the Septuagint to make their argument regarding proper Christian conduct and Israel's fate. For example, the paronomasia for many of the patriarchs' names depend on the Greek text, the work's ethics resonate with arguments made in the Septuagint's wisdom literature, and direct quotations from scripture recite the Greek. Yet the *Testaments'* reliance on the Septuagint for their argument runs much deeper than this short list of superficial connections. In addition to these obvious uses of the Greek text, the *Testaments* echo at a more subtle and significant level the rhetoric of the Septuagint. They occasionally utilize key words, phrases and themes from well-known stories of biblical heroes and villains whose vices and virtues match those discussed by the patriarchs. They also employ, from time to time, the specific language of biblical laws that have a bearing on the patriarchs' behaviours. When a recipient hears the echoes they serve as 'tropes of metalepsis'. That is, not only does the event or law that the echo recalls come to mind, but also the memory of its substance and character as a whole enters the imagination and is integrated with the new composition and its images. For instance, we shall see that the *Testament of Simeon*, on envy, evokes notions of Saul's jealousy for David and Cain's for Abel; and by doing so it adds biblical depth and proportion to its own testimony regarding this key emotion in the Graeco-Roman imagination. With a little care the modern reader can bring to light just these sort of echoes, and by doing so, can also deepen contemporary appreciation of the *Testaments'* particular argument regarding the biblical—thus Jewish and Christian—proportions of a life lived well in the Graeco-Roman world. And with a little imagination the modern reader can see how ancient recipients, more attuned than we are to the rhetoric of the Greek scriptures, would have readily heard the same echoes and have come to similar insights.

Of course, to the modern reader's eye, much of the language in the *Testaments* appears unremarkable and provides little hint of the connections I suggest are there. Hence it takes some work to make the echoes audible, enough labour to make one wonder if what we hear is nothing more than an auditory allusion concocted in the mind of the modern scholar. Even more, one questions whether an ancient author intended the links, and no less so whether ancient audiences perceived them. On these questions we can only be certain that we cannot be certain. But there are protections against pure flights of fancy in locating echoes, safeguards proposed by Richard Hays, the New Testament scholar who originally proposed the search for echoes of Scripture in early Christian literature (1989). Hays suggests that a 'true echo' is one that loosely meets most, if not all of the following criteria. (1) Was the 'proposed source of the echo available to the author and/or original readers?' (2) What is the 'volume' of the echo? Is its language distinctive enough that it would have been recognizable to an ancient audience? (3) Does the echo recur within the writing in which it is located? (4) Is there a thematic coherence between the topic addressed in the target text and the echoed text? (5) Is it plausible that the author of the target text intended the 'alleged meaning effect'? (6) Does the history of interpretation support the perceived echo? Does the same sort of reliance on the echoed text occur elsewhere in Christian or Jewish literature? (7) Does the explanation of the echo 'satisfy' one's exegetical imagination? That is to say, '[d]oes it [the echo] produce for the reader a satisfying account of the effect of the intertextual relation?' (Hays 1989: 29-32). Of course, Hays does not require that every echo identified meet all seven criteria, nor should we. They serve, however, as a broad measure of the plausibility of the intertextual echoes proposed below.

As for the notion that ancient audiences heard the echoes, there can be little doubt. They certainly would have perceived them better than we do. Historians of religion have long pointed out the oral nature of Scripture before the age of Gutenberg. William Graham (1987: 119-40) cites in abundance the evidence that Christians well into the Middle Ages received Scripture almost exclusively as the spoken word; as a consequence they knew its content by sound and memory. Meanwhile, Walter Ong (1982) and others have established the basic characteristics of literature composed for oral presentation, many of which the *Testaments* evince. For example, the *Testaments* use 'aggregative argumentation' and 'redundancy' to develop the double commandment's centrality and they rely on 'situational' accounts and references to 'lived experience' to inculcate their moral perspective. This evidence favours the view that the earliest recipients of the *Testaments* would have readily heard and understood the echoes of Scripture identified in the following pages.

In this chapter, then, I analyse selected 'echoes of Scripture' in the *Testaments*. The scope of the Guide does not permit a complete assessment of the ways in which the rhetoric and themes of the Septuagint turn up in the *Testaments*. The following examples from the testaments of Reuben, Simeon, Judah, Dan and Gad will have to suffice. What these examples suggest is the degree to which echoes of the Septuagint serve as tropes of metalepsis, tropes that not only deepen contemporary appreciation of the *Testaments'* argument, but that may have made the *Testaments'* argument more compelling to ancient recipients as well.

Echoes in the Testament of Reuben

Reuben's speech alludes richly to Scripture. Especially given the testament's preoccupation with sexual restraint, one expects the frequent tropes from Proverbs that express concern for a young man's relations with women (3.10; 4.1, 8; cf. Prov. 6.24-25). Less obvious, but no less significant, are echoes of other stories from Scripture encompassed in the second and third biography-exhortation units identified in Chapter 2 above (3.9-15; 4.1-5).

In 3.9-10 Reuben warns his children against inordinate interest in women and in 3.11-15 he illustrates his point by recalling his encounter with Bilhah (Gen. 35.22; cf. 49.4). James Kugel rightly notes that this account elaborates on 'hooks' in the two biblical passages, and depends in particular on the claim in Gen. 49.4 that Reuben was as 'unstable as water' (Kugel 1995). But when Reuben says that it was the sight of Bilhah bathing that drove him to distraction and rape, we should think not only of Gen. 35.22; 49.4, but also of 2 Sam. 11 and David's seduction (or rape) of Bathsheba. David's response to the sight of Bathsheba purifying herself (2 Sam. 11.2) was like Reuben's to Bilhah bathing, according to the testament: one of uncontrolled lust. Thus 3.9-15 evokes simultaneously the images of Reuben and David as unbridled rapists.

One would be right to question the 'volume' of the echo of David in Reuben's speech if this were all that connects the two. However, the exhortation in 4.1 to 'wander about in characters (ἐν γράμμασι) and with one's flocks', draws the connection between Reuben and David even closer. The former word is taken by Hollander and de Jonge to refer to the books of the law (1985: 99; cf. Josephus, *Ant.* 5.61 [Thackeray *et al.*]). This reading itself would fit with the allusion to *King* David, since according to Deuteronomic law a king should occupy himself with the law only (Deut. 17.19-20). And while most commentators treat the reference to wandering about with one's flocks as a cross-reference to Issachar as the *Testaments'* embodiment of ἁπλότης, 'simplicity', Issachar's simplicity depends on his status as a farmer, *not a shepherd* (*T. Iss.* 3.1, 6; 5.3). David, on the other hand, is a shepherd (1 Sam. 16.11, 19; 17.34 LXX). So, having evoked the memory of the wicked David with the story of Reuben's lust for the bathing Bilhah (3.11-15), the testament points also to the positive portrait of David, the one who, as a shepherd, trusted in God alone (1 Sam. 17.37 LXX).

It takes only a little bit of our own imagination to see how this particular instance of echoing the biblical record might have worked on Jews and Christians in the Graeco-Roman world, were they able to hear the echoes uncovered here. In that socio-historical context self-control and sexual restraint were highly-prized virtues (see, e.g., Isocrates, *On the Peace* 119 [Norlin]; Musonius, *Fragments* 12 [Lutz]), and the way to achieve them was generally thought to be through self-discipline and education of the mind and soul, both of which unfortunately fall prey to self-indulgent behaviour when discipline and control are lacking. The testament agrees that these virtues are to be held in high regard, but it parts ways with the common Hellenistic ethic in asserting that it is not because of the presence or absence of self-discipline that one is vice-ridden or virtuous. Instead, vices are the result of living under the influence of evil spirits (2.1–3.8) and falling into the wily traps of wicked women (5.1–6.4), and virtue is achieved by turning to and trusting in God (4.1). To illustrate the negative point the testament hearkens to David and Bathsheba within Reuben's tale of woe to prove that even the most heroic of figures is subject to the temptations of a woman and the force of evil spirits. At the same time, though, it reminds the reader that David was nonetheless also an honourable and virtuous figure precisely when he was a simple shepherd who relied on God for deliverance (1 Sam. 17.37 LXX). Thus the ancient audience was permitted to accede to the Graeco-Roman definition of a good man on this point, but they were also encouraged to see that the path to such goodness did not begin with self-discipline and education of the mind and soul, but with trust in the God of Israel. Hence recipients would have been granted a way to accommodate to the demands of the dominant culture while maintaining a faithful posture vis-à-vis the God of Israel. In this lies the contribution of the echoes in Reuben's speech to the *Testaments'* larger theological claims.

Echoes in the Testament of Simeon

As noted above, biblical allusions in Simeon's speech surely conjured in the minds of its earliest recipients comparisons between the patriarch's φθόνος, 'envy', for his brother Joseph and that of Saul for David and Cain for Abel. In doing so the testament probably succeeded in steering audiences toward a 'biblicized' understanding of the Graeco-Roman vice of envy, just as Reuben's testament directed recipients toward a theologized notion of self restraint.

Passing acquaintance with Graeco-Roman literature alerts one to the fact that we encounter in the *Testament of Simeon* the familiar Greek *topos* of φθόνος. Plato, Plutarch, Josephus and Dio Chrysostom, to name a few, address this popular theme. The envious person is prone to violence, killing and war (Plato, *Lysis* 215D [Bury *et al.*]; Plutarch, *Moralia* 91B [Babbitt *et al.*]), his friendships wither (Plato, *Philebus* 49D [Bury *et al.*]; Plutarch, *Moralia* 536F [Babbitt *et al.*]), and his envious behaviour spawns a surfeit of associated miseries (see the description of Cain's fate as a result of his envious fratricide in Josephus, *Ant.* 1.56-66 [Thackeray *et al.*]). The cause of envy is an untrained mind. Thus Dio Chrysostom says that the antithesis of the envious person, ὁ ἀνηρ ἀφθόνος, is the ideal philosopher who submits his mind to correction, and he observes that the man without envy seeks the good of others and lives life in a spirit of generosity (Dio Chrysostom, *Discourse* 77/78.39-45 [Cohoon]).

Against this backdrop the testament takes its stand regarding envy by drawing Simeon and Joseph into a comparative relationship with Saul and David and Cain and Abel. First, 2.6-7 compels one to compare Simeon with Saul. While Simeon's confession of jealousy against Joseph and of his resolve to kill him in 2.6-7a recalls Gen. 37.11, 18, 20, 26, *T. Sim.* 2.7b also draws Saul into the orbit of the recipient's imagination. The verse says that the spirit of deceit, who sent upon Simeon a spirit of jealousy, caused his envy. Yet in the biblical narrative about Simeon *no spirit* drives him or his brothers to hate Joseph. So where did this notion come from? The descriptions of Saul in 1 Sam. 18.10; 19.9 provide an answer. Hearing twice of David's exploits on the battlefield and the praise given David over that given himself, Saul is each time overcome by an evil spirit from God that compels him to take violent action against David. So when a spirit is named here as the reason for Simeon's jealousy, it is natural to think of Saul, and all the more so when we see that Josephus preserves a tradition that an evil spirit not associated with God afflicted Saul with precisely the emotion dealt with here, φθόνος (*Ant.* 6.214 [Thackeray *et al.*]).

Testament of Simeon 2.8, 13 may also call to mind Saul's attempt on David's life and God's protection for David as a parallel to Simeon's intent to murder Joseph and God's deliverance of him from his brother's wrath. In 2.8, 12 Simeon says that God delivered Joseph 'from my hands' (ἐκ τῶν χειρῶν μου), and that in recompense for his evil intentions God afflicted his right hand for seven days (ἡ χείρ μου ἡ δεξιὰ ἡμίξηρος ἦν ἐπὶ ἡμέρας ἑπτά). Hollander and de Jonge say that the disability is the *Testaments'* typical view of the punishment for sinful actions: according to *T. Gad* 5.10 one is afflicted in the organ that transgresses (Hollander and de Jonge 1985: 114; see *T. Reub.* 1.7 [a sexual predator is plagued in the loins], and *T. Gad* 5.10 [Gad's liver is beset with illness because he set it against Joseph]). Likewise, Hollander and de Jonge suggest that had Simeon acted against Joseph to kill him he would have used his hands to do so. There is a problem, though. As in the case of Gad's transgression, Simeon's sin was also seated in his liver ('and I set my liver against him to kill him' [2.7]), and he never lifted a hand against his brother; moreover, he later reports that his liver pained him as a result of his anger against Joseph (4.1). Hence the afflicted hand seems superfluous, at least until one remembers Saul who has already been ghosted into the narrative by the references to an evil spirit that afflicts one with envy. In 1 Sam. 18 and 19, where Saul's spirit-induced envy is described, we hear that as a result of his emotions he tried to skewer David with a spear that is pointedly described as resting 'in his hand' (ἐν χείρι αὐτοῦ; 18.10; 19.9); but David was unharmed, because God was with him (18.12). So like Saul, Simeon's hand was denied its natural action because of his ill intent and like David, Joseph was delivered by God's favour for him.

Cain is also echoed in Simeon's autobiographical comments. While Cain is more elusive in the passage than Saul, there can be no doubt that the readers of the *Testaments* would have thought of Cain and Abel alongside Simeon and Joseph. After all, envy is attributed only to Cain as a named individual in the whole of the *Testaments*. *Testament of Benjamin* 7.1-5 reports Cain's submission to the yoke of Beliar and the resulting seven evils his mind conceived, the first of which was envy (φθόνος). Because of the sins he committed against God while under the control of Beliar, Cain suffered seven vengeances over seven hundred years of his life. *Testament of Benamin* 7.5 concludes by saying that it was hatred born of envy that brought all this upon him; likewise any who make the same mistake will also be punished with a similar judgment. It is in this light that one may understand the seven-day affliction of Simeon's right hand (2.12-13a; for a similar inversion of the promise of sevenfold protection/ recompense, see Josephus, *Ant.* 1.58 [Thackeray *et al.*]; Philo, *Quaest. in Gen.* 1.77 [Colson *et al.*]; *T. Benj.* 7.3).

The echoes of Saul and David and Cain and Abel in Simeon's biographical speech surely affected recipients well tutored in the Hebrew Bible. As tropes they conjured for audiences comparisons between Simeon and Joseph, Cain and Abel, and Saul and David. Thus the text compelled the recipients to see that the violence that governed commerce between Israel's first two brothers and first two kings ruled the relationship between these two sons of Jacob, and in all cases the root cause of the tempestuous relationships was envy. Indeed, the last two verses of the biographical section (3.13-14), where φθόνος appears for the first time, hit the reader square in the face with it: Simeon says that because of envy he hated Joseph and plotted to kill him. With those words one is explicitly invited to consider these three biblical accounts as stories about the vice of envy and its effects. And with this invitation the testament has laid a trap, for already it has adjusted the Graeco-Roman notion of how envy begins and how its destructive effects may be suspended. It does not begin with the sickness of a weak and undisciplined mind, but as the consequence of God's rival, Beliar, gaining the upper hand in the battle for the human soul (2.7). And its advance is not stemmed by tutoring the mind, but by weeping, repentance and flight to the Most High God (2.13). So as the text moves on to parenesis it looks like a standard Hellenistic discussion of φθόνος, but with this new twist already set firmly before the reader's mind.

Indeed, apart from the unique elements that set it apart, one could easily mistake the parenetical section of the testament for a classical moralist's discourse on φθόνος. The text describes envy's ability to disturb the mind (3.2; 4.8c, e), generate enmity and violence (3.3a; 4.8a, d), make the body sick (3.3b; 4.1, 8b), deprive one of sleep (4.8g, 9), make good deeds impossible (3.2b; 4.8f), and give one an unappealing appearance (4.1a, 9b). And though the text does not call him a man without envy, by contrast Joseph is described as the epitome of acting generously toward others (4.4-6; 5.1).

The ethical discourse is unique in its claims regarding envy's origin and cure and its association of this notion of envy with Simeon, Saul and Cain, and its opposite with David and Joseph. So 3.1, 5b; 4.7b, 9b; 5.3b-c make clear the responsibility of an evil spirit for generating in human hearts the envious inclination, and 3.4-6 say once again that the remedy for a soul afflicted with envy is flight to God. As for the continued allusions to Saul and Cain as illustrations of envy's troublesome effects, see, for example, the references to a disturbed mind, savage soul and deprivation of sleep in 4.8 and their echoes of biblically-reported conditions that beset Cain and Saul. Likewise, see the claim in 3.2b that the envious person can do no good and its echo of God's words to Cain in Gen. 4.7. The comparison of Joseph with David, on the other hand, is also possible in 5.1 where the description of Joseph as 'comely in appearance and beautiful to look at' does parallel the language used to describe Joseph in Gen. 39.6, but also provides a thematic parallel with the description of David in 1 Sam. 16.12; 17.42. The cumulative effect of this treatment of envy in relationship to these biblical stories would have been to reinforce the point about envy's origin and cure: while Saul and Cain were caught by an evil spirit, failed to flee to God for help, and suffered the consequences, Simeon, though also a victim of the evil spirit, nevertheless sought God's help and escaped.

Notably, the eschatological section (especially 6.2-6) summarizes the testament's point with respect to the theme of θφόνος: embracing this revised view of envy and the ways of escaping it not only creates the individual good enjoyed by Joseph, David or any Gentiles who take the same path; it also leads to the glorification of all Israel and its establishment as a messianic kingdom.

To summarize, we might ask what *theological* notions this testament's echoes of the biblical story conjured for Jewish and Christian readers. First, it is apparent that any reader familiar with the Graeco-Roman *topos* of envy would be tempted to view things differently from most of their fellow citizens as a result of reading the work. The testament drives home the point that envy does not derive from weak human minds, but from the influence of evil spirits, and its effect is not controlled by intellectual self-discipline, but by flight to God. Second, the echoes of Saul and Cain in this framework would have had an apologetic effect for Jews and Christians in relationship to their nonbelieving fellow citizens. It is easy to imagine that the popular judgment of those two figures, in the light of the standard Hellenistic view of envy, would be that they were merely untutored Israelites who lacked intelligence and discipline and so suffered their particular fates. But Simeon's testament nullifies that judgment, showing that their fault lay not in a lack of education and discipline, but in the control Beliar exercised over them. By contrast, Simeon's case shows that through flight to God the believer can more readily escape envy's grasp than can the nonbeliever who thinks it is through self-discipline that one becomes a man without envy. Third, through the closing section of the testament the reader is forced to consider the possibility that trusting God and rejecting the control of Beliar and of envy leads not only to the benefits that accrued to David and Joseph, but also to eschatological fulfilment for the whole community. Thus, for Christian and Jewish readers this testament would have provided a critique of the popular notion that the human person was master over his envy or generosity and that he or she was responsible for creating one's own good or bad reality. It would also have challenged its audience to embrace the alternative notion that it is God or Beliar who is in control, and that flight to God not only brings goodness to the individual, but glory to the elect community when it seeks corporately to live in God's care.

Echoes in the Testament of Judah

Judah's exhortation regarding desire (13.1–19.4) echoes more biblical passages than one at first notices. And like the speeches of all those examined thus far, the echoes work to underscore the *Testaments'* larger argument regarding the concomitance between God's requirements and a Graeco-Roman lifestyle.

Judah begins his exhortation by urging his sons to listen to him and to keep all his words, 'to perform the ordinances of the Lord and to obey the commandment of God' (13.1). This particular combination of terms recalls Deut. 30.15-20 (see especially Deut. 30.16 with its combined use of the words used here for 'ordinance' [ἐντολή] and 'commandment' [δικαιώμα]). Thus in the hearing of this speech one could hardly help but think that heeding Judah's word amounts to fulfilment of the Mosaic law, which, of course, was not yet given by the time of Judah's death, but was nonetheless of concern for early Jewish recipients of the *Testaments*. Then 13.2 goes on to speak of what one must avoid by keeping the ancestor's words, using language that describes two basic vices known to the Graeco-Roman imagination: desire (ἐπιθυμία) and arrogance (ὑπερηφανία). Thus not only does heeding Judah's word fulfil Mosaic law; it also leads away from some of the most basic vices that Graeco-Roman culture counselled one against.

The exhortation then gives specific content to the law that one should keep, and explains how Judah's advice, and the law, will protect one from the vices' evil consequences. In 13.7 Judah indicates that in marrying Bathshua while under the influence of her beauty and wealth and an excess of wine he violated the commandment of his God (Deut. 7.3-4) and his fathers (Gen. 24.3; 26.6, 8). Using the language of Lev. 18.15, the law against intercourse with one's daughter-in-law, Judah says in 14.5 that by his encounter with Tamar he sinned; and in 14.6 he reiterates that he sinned against God's commandment by marrying Bathshua. *Testament of Judah* 18.2-6 then makes clear that the vices can blind one to God's law and its keeping and bring upon one terrible consequences (18.3-5), but if one remains in Judah's word (v. 2b) and heeds the commandments of God (18.6a), the difficulties of a life lived under the influence of impurity and love of money can be avoided. Indeed, says Judah in closing, the ultimate consequence of faithfulness to God and God's law are mercy and freedom from captivity among one's enemies (23.5).

Taken as a whole, Judah's parenesis for his children is like much of what appears otherwise in the *Testaments*: it uses the common rhetoric of Graeco-Roman moralist discourse to promote a notion of the well-led life, but it instructs one on such an existence with biblical rhetoric. Avoiding the bad consequences of inordinate desire is possible by living according to the instructions Judah, his brothers and his fathers before him gave; and those instructions, as it turns out, are identical with the Mosaic law in large (13.1=Deut. 30.16) and small (13.7=Deut. 7.3-4; 14.5=Lev. 18.15) ways.

It is also possible that the recipients of the *Testaments*, having already been led by the testaments of Reuben and Simeon to think of David as a positive and negative example, would think again of David as proof of the troubles that come from allowing one's desire to rule. The connection, after all, would be quite natural: just as Judah is lured into an ill-fated marriage by the beauty of a woman named Bathshua (1 Chron. 2.3), and produces from that marriage children that die by God's hand (Gen. 38.7, 10), David also is forced into marriage because of his lack of control at the sight of a beautiful woman called Bathshua (1 Chron. 3.5) and produces from the union a child fated by God to die (2 Sam. 12.14, 18). So not only is the recipient of the *Testaments* compelled to see in the biblical David an example of the tragedies that befall anyone who is afflicted by the Graeco-Roman vice of inordinate desire; he or she is also encouraged to understand that it is God who punishes the human who gives in to unrestrained lust.

Echoes in the Testament of Dan

The *Testament of Dan* dwells on the anger Dan felt toward his brother Joseph. Because the Bible reveals so little about the patriarch, the *Testaments*' authors were apparently forced to recount his story from bits of Scripture relating to the descendants of Dan. There are few Danites more famous than Samson, so it is not surprising that the principal figure echoed in this testament is that well-known judge.

First, in a very general sense one may say that the theme of the testament recalls Samson. He was, like his forefather Dan in the testament's account, afflicted with an occasionally irrational anger. The Bible speaks explicitly about his rage after he lost his bet with the Philistine men of Timnah regarding the riddle (Judg. 14.12-20). Judg. 14.19 LXX states that Samson's anger (θυμός) at losing the bet drove him to act rashly in his attack on innocent Ashkelon. He even admits that he was not entirely just on this occasion when he says about a second round of mischief against Philistia that 'this time' he will be without blame (15.3). The implication, of course, is that Samson exercised less than good judgment in his actions in the earlier incident. Likewise, the testament recounts Dan's unjust and senseless anger against Joseph. His jealousy drove him to plan violence that, save for God's protection of Joseph, would have terminated his brother's line.

Another text provides a much more specific allusion to Samson. Anticipating his descendants' future, Dan says in 5.5 that they will 'act impurely with the women of the lawless ones'. The behaviour implied by Dan's exhortation is clearly intercourse with non-Israelites. While such unions are addressed already in *T. Levi* 9.10; *T. Jud.* 13.7; 14.6, this reference seems to come from nowhere. Isaac's insistence that Levi not marry a Gentile probably comes from the Levi tradition evident in the Aramaic source material, and the concern for marriage with non-Jews is natural in the *Testament of Judah*, preoccupied as it is with the difficulties that women—particularly non-Israelite women—engender for men. But in *T. Dan* 5.5 there is simply no context for the comment; rather, it comes suddenly as a future sin of Dan's descendants, one that seems unrelated to his own history. Thus one is driven outside of the story world to locate a reason for Dan's claim against his children. One need look no further than Samson. Judges 14.1–15.20 tells the story of his fateful marriage to the Philistine woman in Timnah; 16.1-3 recounts the tale of his encounter with the prostitute at Gaza and the locals' attempt on that occasion to destroy him; and, of course, there is the story of his marriage to the 'flirt' Deliliah, whose name would indicate her non-Israelite birth (although the valley of Sorek could have been the home of Gentiles or Israelites).

One final echo of Scripture is worth noting in the *Testament of Dan*. Dan notes that it was a spirit of anger that tried to convince him to 'suck out Joseph as a leopard sucks out a lamb' (1.8). The use of ἐκμύζαω, 'to suck out', is puzzling (see Charles 1908b: 124, for a suggested alternative reading that would allow one translate the word as 'crush'), but the reference to a leopard and a lamb in one phrase is unmistakable: it recalls, and suggests the near reversal of, the messianic prediction passage of Isa. 11.1-9 (see v. 6). Thus in this case we encounter an oblique, and seemingly unnoticed, Joseph-as-type-of-Jesus passage.

Echoes in the Testament of Gad

A brief passage in *T. Gad* 1.6-9 once again draws the images of David and Saul into view, but this time in the person of one individual. Gad tells his children that Joseph's bad report to Jacob about the sons of Zilpah and Bilhah (Gen. 37.2) was a misrepresentation of a larger incident. Joseph told his father that Gad and his brothers were killing and eating the best of the flock. Gad echoes David when he corrects Joseph's report, saying in 1.7 that what Joseph saw was only part of a larger act: a bear had attacked a lamb and Gad had ripped the unfortunate beast from the bear's jaws, killed the bear, and dispatched the mortally wounded lamb, only later to consume it so as not to let it go to waste (cf. 1.2-3). His account of the event is almost heavy-handed in its mirroring of David's claim before Saul that his past experience as a bear-slaying shepherd qualified him to take on Goliath (1 Sam. 17.34-36). But then in 1.8-9 Gad goes on to say how Joseph's injustice against him made him indignant (1.8) and planted in him a spirit of anger against Joseph so intense that he neither wished to see or hear Joseph anymore (1.9). The last sequence recalls Saul. When he found cause to be jealous of David (1 Sam. 18.7), he also became angry (18.8) and fell under the spell of a wicked spirit that created in him a murderous intent (18.10-11) and caused him to put David out of his sight and hearing (18.13). And just as David prospered all the more after his removal from Saul's presence because God was with him (18.14-16), Joseph came to power and wealth after Gad's rejection of him because God blessed him (*T. Jos.* 1.2-7). Thus the hearer of this passage from the *Testament of Gad* could hardly help but recognize the ways in which Gad's ambiguous position in relationship to Joseph is related to biblical figures. He is likened to David for his valour and quick action on behalf of his father's flocks, and so his image in the recipient's mind is given real lustre. But his indulgence in the vices of jealousy and hatred makes him a less sympathetic figure, and so he is likened as well to David's nemesis, Saul, also an infamous victim of the envy and rage. By evoking the conflicting emotive responses to hearing the stories of David and Saul, the testament summons the same sentiments regarding Gad. Surely that is appropriate in Gad's case, since his vice, though regrettable and a legitimate matter of concern for the testament, was actually prompted by the unjust behaviour of his otherwise nearly perfect brother Joseph.

Concluding Remarks

This Guide set out, in part, to demonstrate the ways in which the *Testaments* would have been perceived by Christian *and* Jewish recipients to argue for the equivalence between the instruction of the patriarchs, general standards of good behaviour in the Graeco-Roman world, and the life and teachings of Jesus the messiah. Ancient audiences would have also perceived an argument that adhering to the teachings of the patriarchs and embracing Jesus as messiah were equal acts. As such the *Testaments* can best be understood, in their present form, as a Christian composition that addressed Christians and Jews living in the Graeco-Roman world. The *Testaments* testified that one could fit into the surrounding culture while confessing Jesus as messiah, and that doing both things could be accomplished within the framework of the teachings of Israel's ancestors. Furthermore the Guide has argued that that the *Testaments'* agenda is furthered by their generous use of biblical, especially septuagintal, rhetoric. Whether the authors of the work intended the echoes of biblical heroes and villains whose lives demonstrated the virtues and vices addressed by the Testaments cannot be determined. Nonetheless, the ancient recipients of the *Testaments* probably heard those echoes, and in appreciating them they were provided further encouragement to embrace the *Testaments'* vision as true to their biblical heritage, and worthy of their intellectual and spiritual assent.

Further Reading

Few have devoted much attention to the more subtle echoes of Scripture in the *Testaments*. There is, however, the substantial and fascinating work of James Kugel (1992, 1993, 1995), supplemented in a grand way now by his recent treatment of early Jewish and Christian interpretations of the biblical motifs. Published in popular (1997) and scholarly (1998) editions, this masterful compendium of later readings of biblical themes is devoted in large part to postbiblical treatments of the ancestral stories. In addition, as noted in 'Further Reading' for Chapter 2, Kugel will write the commentary on the *Testaments* for the Hermeneia series. Of course, Hollander and de Jonge (1985) remains the essential starting point for any further study along these lines; their notes are an incredibly rich mine of citations to related Jewish and Christian texts that point one in many possible directions in the search for echoes of Scripture in the *Testaments*. Their work, in fact, provided the basis for much of what I develop here.

For the notion of echoes of Scripture in later writings, see Hays (1989) and J. Hollander (1981). And for orality and literacy in relationship to Scripture, see Graham (1987) and Ong (1982).

Bibliography

Amstutz, J.
    1968   *ΑΠΛΟΤΗΣ: Eine begriffsgeschichtliche Studie zum jüdisch-christlichen Griechisch* (Theophaneia, 19; Bonn: P. Hanstein).

Argyle, A.W.
    1952   'The Influence of the Testaments of the Twelve Patriarchs on the New Testament', *ExpTim* 63: 256-58.
    1955–56 'Joseph the Patriarch in Patristic Teaching', *ExpTim* 67: 199-201.

Aschermann, P.H.
    1955   'Die paränetischen Formen der "Testamente der zwölf Patriarchen" und ihr Nachwirken in der frühchristlichen Mahnung' (ThD dissertation, Humboldt-Universität-Berlin).

Aschim, A.
    1998   'Review of *From Patriarch to Priest: The Levi Priestly Tradition from Aramaic Levi to the Testament of Levi*', *JBL* 117: 353-55.

Audet, J.-P.
    1952   'Affinités littéraires et doctrinales du Manuel de discipline', *RB* 59: 219-38.
    1953   'Affinités littéraires et doctrinales du Manuel de discipline', *RB* 60: 41-82.

Baarda, T.
    1988   'Qehath—"What's in a Name?" Concerning the Interpretation of the Name "Qehath" in the Testament of Levi 11:4-6', *JSJ* 19: 215-29.
    1992   'The Shechem Episode in the Testament of Levi: A Comparison with Other Traditions', in J.N. Bremmer and Florentino García Martínez (eds.), *Sacred History and Sacred Text* (Kampen: Pharos): 11-73.

Babbitt, F.C. *et al.*
    1927–76 *Plutarch's Moralia* (15 vols.; LCL; Cambridge, MA: Harvard University Press).

Baltzer, K.
    1960   *Das Bundesformular* (WMANT, 4; Neukirchen–Vluyn: Neukirchener Verlag).

Barthélemy, D., and J.T. Milik
    1955   *Discoveries in the Judaean Desert 1* (Oxford: Clarendon Press).

Barton, J.
    1986   *The Oracles of God: Perceptions of Ancient Prophecy in Israel after the Exile* (New York: Oxford University Press).

Beasley-Murray, G.R.
    1947   'The Two Messiahs in the Testaments of the Twelve Patriarchs', *JTS* 48: 1-12.

Becker, J.
1970　　　*Untersuchungen zur Entstehungsgeschichte der Testamente der Zwölf Patriarchen* (AGJU, VIII; Leiden: E.J. Brill).
1974　　　*Unterweisung in lehrhafter Form* (JSHRZ, 3; Gütersloh: Gerd Mohn).
Beyer, K.
1984　　　*Die aramäischen Texten vom Toten Meer* (Göttingen: Vandenhoeck & Ruprecht): 188-208.
1994　　　*Die aramäischen Texten vom Toten Meer: Ergänzungsband* (Göttingen: Vandenhoeck & Ruprecht): 71-78.
Bickerman, E.
1950　　　'The Date of the Testaments of the Twelve Patriarchs', *JBL* 69: 245-60.
Braun, F.-C.
1960　　　'Les Testaments des XII Patriarches et le problème de leur origine', *RB* 67: 516-49.
Braun, F.M.
1938　　　*History and Romance in Graeco-Roman Literature* (Oxford: Blackwell).
Brooke, G. *et al.*
1996　　　*Qumran Cave 4, XVIII: Parabiblical Texts, Part 3* (DJD, 22; Oxford: Clarendon Press): 1-82.
Bruce, B.
1990　　　*Origen's Homilies on Joshua: An Annotated Translation* (Ann Arbor, MI [Dissertation, Southern Baptist Theological Seminary, 1988]).
Burchard, C.
1969　　　'Zur armenischen Überlieferung der Testamente der zwölf Patriarchen', in Eltester (ed.) 1969: 1-29.
1985　　　'Joseph and Aseneth', in Charlesworth (ed.) 1985: II, 177-248.
Bury, R.G. *et al.*
1967-82　　*Plato* (12 vols.; LCL; Cambridge, MA: Harvard University Press).
Caquot, A.
1972　　　'La double investiture de Lévi', *SHR* (=Supp. to *Numen*) 21: 156-61.
Charles, R.H.
1908a　　　*The Greek Versions of the Testaments of the Twelve Patriarchs* (Oxford: Oxford University Press).
1908b　　　*The Testaments of the Twelve Patriarchs: Translated from the Editor's Greek Text* (London: Blackwell).
1913　　　*The Apocrypha and Pseudepigrapha of the Old Testament in English* (Oxford: Clarendon Press): II, 282-367.
Charles, R.H., and A. Cowley
1907　　　'An Early Source of the Testaments of the Patriarchs', *JQR* 19: 566-83.
Charlesworth, J.H.
1985　　　'More Psalms of David', in Charlesworth (ed.) 1985: II, 609-24.
Charlesworth, J.H. (ed.)
1983, 1985　*The Old Testament Pseudepigrapha* (2 vols.; New York: Doubleday).
Chevallier, M.-A.
1958　　　*L'esprit et le messie dans le bas judaïsme et le Nouveau Testament* (Paris: Presses universitaires de France).

Clarke, E.G.
1998   *Targum Pseudo-Jonathan, Deuteronomy* (The Aramaic Bible, 5B; Wilming-
           ton, DE: Liturgical Press).
Cohoon, J.W.
1932–51   *Dio Chrysostom* (5 vols.; LCL; Cambridge, MA: Harvard University
           Press).
Collins, J.J.
1983   *Between Athens and Jerusalem: Jewish Identity in the Hellenistic Diaspora*
           (New York: Crossroad).
1984   'Testaments', in Michael Stone (ed.), *Jewish Writings of the Second Temple
           Period: Apocrypha, Pseudepigrapha, Qumran Sectarian Writings, Philo,
           Josephus* (CRINT, II.2; Assen: Van Gorcum; Philadelphia: Fortress
           Press): 325-55.
1987   'The Kingdom of God in the Apocrypha and Pseudepigrapha', in
           Wendell Willis (ed.), *The Kingdom of God in 20th-Century Interpretation*
           (Peabody, MA: Hendrickson): 81-95.
1995   *The Scepter and the Star: The Messiahs of the Dead Sea Scrolls and Other
           Ancient Literature* (ABRL; New York: Doubleday).
1998   *The Apocalyptic Imagination: An Introduction to Jewish Apocalyptic Literature*
           (Grand Rapids, MI: Eerdmans, 2nd edn).
Colson, F.H. *et al.*
1929–62   *Philo* (12 vols.; LCL; Cambridge, MA: Harvard University Press).
Conybeare, F.C.
1893   'On the Jewish Authorship of the Testaments of the Twelve Patriarchs',
           JQR 5: 375-95.
Cortès, E.
1976   *Los discursos deadiós de Gn 49 a Jn 13–17: pistas para la historia de un género
           literario en la antigua literatura judía* (Barcelona: Herder).
Dupont-Sommer, A.
1951–52   'Le Testament de Lévi (XVII-XVIII) et la secte juive de l'Alliance',
           Semitica 4: 33-53.
1953   *Nouveaux aperçus sur les manuscrits de la mer morte* (Paris: Maisonneuve).
Eltester, W.
1969   *Studien zu den Testamenten der Zwölf Patriarchen* (Berlin: Töpelmann).
Eppel, R.
1930   *Le piétisme juif dans les Testaments de douze patriarches* (Paris: Félix Alcan).
Ewald, M.L.
1966   *The Homilies of Saint Jerome*, II (2 vols.; The Fathers of the Church, 57;
           Washington, DC: Catholic University of America Press).
Falls, T.B.
1948   *Writings of Saint Justin Martyr* (The Fathers of the Church, 6; Washing-
           ton, DC: Catholic University of America Press).
Ferguson, E.
1993   *Backgrounds of Early Christianity* (Grand Rapids, MI: Eerdmans, 2nd
           edn).
Frazier, G.
1921   *Apollodorus, The Library* (LCL; Cambridge, MA: Harvard University
           Press).

Gaster, M.
   1894   'The Hebrew Text of One of the Testaments of the Twelve Patriarchs',
               Society of Biblical Archeology: Proceedings 16-17: 33-49.
Gaylord, H.E., and Th. Korteweg
   1975   'The Slavic Versions', in de Jonge (ed.) 1975: 140-43.
Ginzberg, L.
   1909–38   *The Legends of the Jews* (7 vols.; Philadelphia: Jewish Publication Society).
Grabe, J.E.
   1698   *Spicilegium SS. Patrum ut et Haereticorum, seculi post Christum natum I, II, &*
               III (2 vols.; Oxford, n.p.).
Graham, W.
   1987   *Beyond the Written Word: Oral Aspects of Scripture in the History of Religion*
               (Cambridge: Cambridge University Press).
Greenfield, J., and M. Stone
   1979   'Remarks on the Aramaic Testament of Levi from the Geniza', *RB* 86:
               216-30.
   1985   'Appendix III: The Aramaic and Greek Fragments of a Levi Document',
               in Hollander and de Jonge 1985: 457-69.
Grelot, P.
   1956   'Notes sur le Testament araméen de Lévi', *RB* 63: 391-406.
   1971   'Quatre cents trente ans (Ex XII, 40): du Pentateuque au Testament
               araméen de Lévi', in A. Caquot and M. Philonenko (eds.), *Hommages à*
               André Dupont-Sommer (Paris: Adrien-Maisonneuve): 383-94.
   1975   'Quatre cents trente ans (Ex 12,40): du Testament de Lévi aux visions
               de 'Amram', in Alvarez Verdes (ed.), *Homenaje a Juan Prado* (Madrid:
               Consejo Superior): 559-70.
   1981   'Le Livre des Jubilés et le Testament de Lévi', in P. Casetti, O. Keel and
               Adrian Schenker (eds.), *Mélanges Dominique Barthélemy: Etudes bibliques*
               offertes a l'occasion de son 60e anniversaire (OBO, 38; Göttingen: Vanden-
               hoeck & Ruprecht): 110-33.
Haupt, D.
   1969   'Das Testament des Levi: Untersuchungen zu seiner Entstehung und
               Überlieferungsgeschichte' (ThD dissertation, Halle-Wittenberg).
Hays, R.
   1989   *Echoes of Scripture in the Letters of Paul* (New Haven, CT: Yale University
               Press).
Hengel, M.
   1974   *Judaism and Hellenism* (Philadelphia: Fortress Press).
Higgins, A.J.B.
   1953   'Priest and Messiah', *VT* 3: 321-28.
   1966–67   'The Priestly Messiah', *NTS* 13: 211-39.
Hilgert, E.
   1985   'The Dual Image of Joseph in Hebrew and Early Jewish Literature',
               Papers of the Chicago Society of Biblical Research 30: 5-21.
   1986   '"By the Sea of Jamnia", *TNaph* 6:1', in A. Caquot, M. Hadas-Lebel and
               J. Riaud (eds.), *Hellenica et Judaica* (Leuven: Peeters): 245-55.

Hollander, H.W.
1981   *Joseph as an Ethical Model in the Testaments of the Twelve Patriarchs* (SVTP,
        6; Leiden: E.J. Brill).
Hollander, H.W., and M. de Jonge
1985   *The Testaments of the Twelve Patriarchs: A Commentary* (SVTP, 8; Leiden:
        E.J. Brill).
Hollander, J.
1981   *The Figure of Echo: A Mode of Allusion in Milton and After* (Berkeley, CA:
        University of California Press).
Hultgård, A.
1977   *L'eschatologie des Testaments des Douze Patriarches. I. Interpretation des textes*
        (Acta Universitatis Upsaliensis, Historia Religionum, 6; Uppsala: Alm-
        qvist & Wiksell).
1980   'The Ideal "Levite", the Davidic Messiah, and the Saviour Priest in the
        Testaments of the Twelve Patriarchs', in John J. Collins and G.W.E.
        Nickelsburg (eds.), *Ideal Figures in Ancient Judaism* (Chico, CA: Scholars
        Press): 93-100.
1982   *L'eschatologie des Testaments des Douze Patriarches. II. Composition de
        l'ouvrage; textes et traductions* (Acta Universitatis Upsaliensis, Historia
        Religionum, 7; Uppsala: Almqvist & Wiksell).
Hunkin, J.W.
1914   'The Testaments of the Twelve Patriarchs', *JTS* 16: 80-97.
Jervell, J.
1969   'Ein Interpolator interpretiert: Zu der christlichen Bearbeitung der
        Testamente der zwölf Patriarchen', in Eltester 1969: 30-61.
Jonge, H.J. de
1975a   'The Earliest Traceable Stage of the Textual Tradition of the Testa-
        ments of the Twelve Patriarchs', in de Jonge (ed.) 1975: 63-86.
1975b   'Die Patriarchentestamente von Roger Bacon bis Richard Simon', in de
        Jonge (ed.) 1975: 3-42.
Jonge, M. de
1953   *The Testaments of the Twelve Patriarchs: A Study of their Text, Composition,
        and Origin* (Assen: Van Gorcum).
1960   'Christian Influence in the Testaments of the Twelve Patriarchs', *NovT*
        4: 182-235.
1962   'Once More: Christian Influence on the Testaments of the Twelve
        Patriarchs', *NovT* 5: 311-19.
1975a   'The Greek Testament of the Twelve Patriarchs and the Armenian
        Version', in de Jonge (ed.) 1975: 120-39.
1975b   'The Interpretation of the Testaments of the Twelve Patriarchs in
        Recent Years', in de Jonge (ed.) 1975: 183-92.
1975c   'Notes on Testament of Levi II-VII', in de Jonge (ed.) 1975: 247-60.
1975d   'Testament Issacahr als "typisches" Testament', in de Jonge (ed.) 1975:
        291-316.
1981   'Levi, the sons of Levi and the Law in *Testament Levi* X, XIV-XV and
        XVI', in J. Doré *et al.* (eds.), *De la Tôrah au Messie: Mélanges H. Cazelles*
        (Paris: Desclée & Cie): 513-23.

1985a   'Hippolytus' "Benediction of Isaac, Jacob and Moses" and the Testaments of the Twelve Patriarchs', *Bijdragen, tijdschrift voor folosofie en theologie* 46: 245-60 (repr. in de Jonge 1991a: 204-19).

1985b   'The Pre-Mosaic Servants of God in the Testaments of the Twelve Patriarchs and in the Writings of Justin and Irenaeus', *VC* 39: 157-70 (repr. in de Jonge 1991a: 263-76).

1985c   'The Testaments of the Twelve Patriarchs: Christian and Jewish. A Hundred Years after Friedrich Schnapp', *NedTTs* 39: 265-75 (repr. in de Jonge 1991a: 233-43).

1986a   'The Future of Israel in the Testaments of the Twelve Patriarchs', *JSJ* 17: 196-211 (repr. in de Jonge 1991a: 164-79).

1986b   'Two Messiahs in the Testaments of the Twelve Patriarchs?', in J.W. van Henten, H.J. de Jonge, P.T. van Rooden and J.W. Wesselius (eds.), *Tradition and Re-Interpretation in Jewish and Early Christians Literature* (Leiden: E.J. Brill): 150-62 (repr. in de Jonge 1991a: 191-203).

1987   'The Testaments of the Twelve Patriarchs: Central Problems and Essential Viewpoints', in *ANRW* II.20.1: 359-420.

1988   'The Testament of Levi and "Aramaic Levi"', *RevQ* 13: 367-85 (repr. in de Jonge 1991a: 180-90).

1989a   'Die Paränese in der Schriften des Neuen Testaments und in de Testamenten der Zwölf Patriarchen', in H. Merklein (ed.), *Neues Testament und Ethik* (Freiburg: Herder, 1989): 538-50.

1989b   'Test. Benjamin 3:8 and the Picture of Joseph as "A Good and Holy Man"', in J.W. van Henten (ed.), *Die Entstehung der jüdischen Martyrologie* (Leiden: E.J. Brill, 1989): 204-14.

1990   'Rachel's Virtuous Behavior in the *Testament of Issachar*', in D. Balch, E. Ferguson and W. Meeks (eds.), *Greeks, Romans, and Christians: Essays in Honor of Abraham J. Malherbe* (Minneapolis, MN: Fortress Press, 1990): 340-52.

1991a   *Jewish Eschatology, Early Christian Christology, and the Testaments of the Twelve Patriarchs: Collected Essays of Marinus de Jonge* (SNT, 63; Leiden: E.J. Brill).

1991b   'Robert Grosseteste and the Testaments of the Twelve Patriarchs', *JTS* NS 42: 115-25.

1992   'Patriarchs, Testaments of the Twelve', *ABD*, II: 181-86.

1993   'The Transmission of the Testament of the Twelve Patriarchs by Christians', *VC* 47: 1-28.

1995   'Light on Paul from the *Testaments of the Twelve Patriarchs*?', in L. Michael White and O. Larry Yarbrough (eds.), *The Social World of the First Christians: Essays in Honor of Wayne A. Meeks* (Minneapolis: Fortress Press): 100-15.

1999   'Levi in Aramaic Levi and in the Testament of Levi', in E. Chazon and M. Stone (eds.), *Pseudepigraphic Perspectives: The Apocrypha and Pseudepigrapha in Light of the Dead Sea Scrolls* (Leiden: E.J. Brill): 71-89.

Jonge, M. de (ed.)

1975   *Studies in the Testaments of the Twelve Patriarchs: Text and Interpretation* (SVTP, 3; Leiden: E.J. Brill).

Jonge, M. de, *et al.*
    1978   *The Testaments of the Twelve Patriarchs: A Critical Edition of the Greek Text* (PsVTGr, I, 2; Leiden: E.J. Brill).

Kee, H.C.
    1978   'The Ethical Dimensions of the Testaments of the XII as a Clue to Provenance', *NTS* 24: 259-70.
    1983   'Testaments of the Twelve Patriarchs', in Charlesworth (ed.) 1983: I, 775-828.

Knibb, M.
    1998   'Perspectives on the Apocrypha and Psuedepigrapha: The Levi Traditions', in F. García Martínez and Ed Noort (eds.), *Perspectives in the Study of the Old Testament and Early Judaism: A Symposium in Honour of Adam S. Van der Woude on the Occasion of His 70th Birthday* (Leiden: E.J. Brill): 197-213.

Kolenkow, A.B.
    1975   'The Genre Testament and Forecasts of the Future in the Hellenistic Jewish Milieu', *JSJ* 6: 57-71.

Korteweg, Th.
    1975   'The Meaning of Naphtali's Visions', in de Jonge (ed.) 1975: 161-73.

Küchler, M.
    1979   *Fruhjüdische Weisheitstraditionen* (OBO, 26; Göttingen: Vandehoeck & Ruprecht).

Kugel, J.
    1992   'The Story of Dinah in the *Testament of Levi*', *HTR* 85: 1-34.
    1993   'Levi's Elevation to the Priesthood in Second Temple Writings', *HTR* 86: 1-64.
    1995   'Reuben's Sin with Bilhah in the *Testament of Reuben*', in David P. Wright, David Noel Freedman and Avi Hurvitz (eds.), *Pomegranates and Golden Bells: Studies in Biblical, Jewish, and Near Eastern Ritual, Law, and Literature in Honor of Jacob Milgrom* (Winona Lake, IN: Eisenbrauns): 525-54.
    1997   *The Bible as It Was* (Cambridge, MA: Harvard University Press).
    1998   *Traditions of the Bible: A Guide to the Bible as it Was at the Start of the Common Era* (Cambridge, MA: Harvard University Press).

Kugler, R.
    1996a   *From Patriarch to Priest: The Levi-Priestly Tradition from Aramaic Levi to Testament of Levi* (SBLEJL, 9; Atlanta: Scholars Press).
    1996b   'Some Further Evidence for the Samaritan Provenance of *Aramaic Levi (1QTestLevi; 4QtestLevi)*', *RevQ* 65-68: 351-58.

Kuhn, K.G.
    1952   'Jesus in Gethsemane', *EvT* 12: 260-85.

Lagrange, M.-J.
    1931   *Le judaïsme avant Jésus-Christ* (Paris: Lecoffre).

Lake, K.
    1912   *The Apostolic Fathers* (2 vols.; LCL; London: Heinemann).

Long, A.A., and D.N. Sedley
    1987   *The Hellenistic Philosophers.* I. *Translations of the Principal Sources with Philosophical Commentary* (Cambridge: Cambridge University Press).

Lutz, C.E.
 1990   *Musonius Rufus, 'the Roman Socrates': Greek Text and English Translation*
          (Yale Classical Studies; New Haven, CT: Yale University Press).
McNamara, M.
 1992   *Targum Neofiti, Genesis* (The Aramaic Bible, 1A; Wilmington, DE: Litur-
          gical Press).
Macky, P.
 1969   'The Importance of the Teaching on God, Evil, and Eschatology for
          Dating the Testaments of the Twelve Patriarchs' (ThD dissertation,
          Princeton Theological Seminary).
Maher, M.
 1992   *Targum Pseudo-Jonathan, Genesis* (The Aramaic Bible, 1B; Wilmington,
          DE: Liturgical Press).
Messel, N.
 1918   'Über die textkritisch begründete Ausscheidung vermutlicher christ-
          licher Interpolationen in den Testaments der zwölf Patriarchen', in
          W. Frankenberg and F. Küchler (eds.), *Abhandlungen zur semitischen
          Religionskunde und Sprachwissenschaft* (BZAW, 33; Giessen: Töpelmann):
          355-74.
Milik, J.T.
 1955   'Le Testament de Lévi en araméen: Fragment de la Grotte 4 de
          Qumrân', *RB* 62: 398-406.
 1972   'Milkî-ṣedeq et milkî-reša' dans les anciens écrits juifs et chrétiens', *JJS*
          28: 95-144.
 1978   'Écrits préesséniens de Qumrân; d'Hénoch à 'Amram', in M. Delcor
          (ed.), *Qumrân: Sa piété, sa théologie et son milieu* (BEThL, 46; Gembloux:
          Duculot): 91-106.
Munck, J.
 1950   'Discours d'adieu dans le Nouveau Testament et dans la littérature
          biblique', in *Aux sources de la tradition chrétienne: Festschrift Maurice Goguel*
          (Neuchâtel and Paris: Delachaux & Nestlé): 155-70.
Nebe, G.W.
 1994   'Qumranica I: zu unveröffentlichten Handschriften aus Höhle 4 von
          Qumran', *ZAW* 106: 307-22.
Neusner, J.
 1985   *Genesis Rabbah: The Judaic Commentary to the Book of Genesis* (3 vols.; BJS,
          104-106; Atlanta: Scholars Press).
Nickelsburg, G.W.E. (ed.)
 1975   *Studies on the Testament of Joseph* (SBLSCS, 5; Missoula, MT: Scholars
          Press).
Nickelsburg, G.W.E., and M. Stone
 1983   *Faith and Piety in Early Judaism* (Philadelphia: Fortress Press).
Niehoff, M.
 1992   *The Figure of Joseph in Post-Biblical Jewish Literature* (AGJU, 16; Leiden:
          E.J. Brill).
Nordheim, E. von
 1980   *Die Lehre der Alten. I. Das Testament als Literaturgattung im Judentum der
          hellenistisch-römischen Zeit* (ALGHJ, 13; Leiden: E.J. Brill).

Norlin, G.
    1956   *Isocrates* (LCL; Cambridge, MA: Harvard University Press).

Oldfather, W.A.
    1956   *Epictetus: The Discourses as Repeated by Arrian, the Manual, and Fragments* (2 vols.; LCL; Cambridge, MA: Harvard University Press).

Ong, W.
    1982   *Orality and Literacy: The Technologizing of the Word* (New York: Methuen).

Otzen, B.
    1953   'Die neugefundenen hebräischen Sektenschriften und die Testamente der zwölf Patriarchen', *ST* 7: 125-57.

Pass, H.L., and J. Arendzen
    1900   'Fragment of an Aramaic Text of the Testament of Levi', *JQR* 12: 651-61.

Perry, B.E.
    1965   *Babrius and Phaedrus* (LCL; Cambridge, MA: Harvard University Press).

Pervo, R.
    1975   'The Testament of Joseph and Greek Romance', in Nickelsburg (ed.) 1975: 15-28.

Philonenko, M.
    1960   *Les interpoliations chrétiennes des Testaments des Douze Patriarches et les manuscrits de Qoumrân* (Paris: Presses universitaires de France).
    1970   'Juda et Héraklès', *RHPR* 50: 61-62.
    1979   'Paradoxes Stoïciens dans le Testament de Lévi', in E. Jacob (ed.), *Sagesse et Religion* (Paris: Bibliothèque des centres d'études supérieures spécialés): 99-104.

Porter, J.R.
    1949–50   'The Messiah in the Testament of Levi XVIII', *ExpTim* 61: 90-91.

Puech, E.
    1993   'Fragments d'un apocryphe de Lévi et le personnage eschatologique. 4QTestLévi^{c-d}(?) et 4QAJa$_2$', in J. Trebolle Barrera and L. Vegas Montaner (eds.), *The Madrid Congress: Proceedings of the International Congress on the Dead Sea Scrolls, Madrid 18–21 March 1991* (2 vols.; STDJ, 11; Leiden: E.J. Brill), II: 449-501.

Rabin, C.
    1952   'The "Teacher of Righteousness" in the "Testaments of the Twelve Patriarchs"?', *JJS* 3: 127-28.

Rengstorf, K.H.
    1974   'Herkunft und Sinn der Patriarchen-Reden in den Testamenten der Zwölf Patriarchen', in W.C. van Unnik (ed.), *La littérature juive entre Tenach et Mischna: Quelques problèmes* (Leiden: E.J. Brill): 29-47.

Rosner, B.
    1992   'A Possible Quotation of Test. Reuben 5.5 in 1 Corinthians 6.18A', *JTS* (NS) 43: 123-27.

Schnapp, F.
    1884   *Die Testamente der zwölf Patriarchen untersucht* (Halle: Max Niemeyer).

Slingerland, D.
    1977   *The Testaments of the Twelve Patriarchs: A Critical History of Research* (SBLMS, 21; Missoula, MT: Scholars Press).

1984   'The Levitical Hallmark within the Testaments of the Twelve Patri-
          archs', *JBL* 103: 531-37.
1986   'The Nature of *Nomos* (Law) with the *Testaments of the Twelve Patriarchs*',
          JBL 105: 39-48.
Sparks, H.F.D. (ed.)
1984   *The Apocryphal Old Testament* (Oxford: Clarendon Press).
Steck, O.H.
1967   *Israel und das gewaltsame Geschick der Propheten: Untersuchungen zur Über-
          lieferung des deuteronomischen Geschictsbildes im Alten Testament, Spät-
          judentum und Urchistentum* (Neukirchen–Vluyn: Neukirchener Verlag).
Stewart, R.A.
1967–68   'The Sinless High Priest', *NTS* 14: 126-35.
Stone, M.
1969   *The Testament of Levi: A First Study of the Armenian Manuscripts of the
          Testaments of the XII Patriarchs in the Convent of St. James, Jerusalem, with
          Text, Critical Apparatus, Notes and Translation* (Jerusalem: St. James).
1977   'New Evidence for the Armenian Version of the Testaments of the
          Twelve Patriarchs', *RB* 84: 94-107.
1988a   'Enoch, Aramaic Levi and Sectarian Origins', *JSJ* 19: 159-70.
1988b   'Ideal Figures and Social Context: Priest and Sage in the Early Second
          Temple Age', in P.D. Miller, P.D. Hanson and D.S. McBride (eds.),
          Ancient Israelite Religion (Minneapolis: Fortress Press): 575-86.
1991   'The Epitome of the Testaments of the Twelve Patriarchs', in M.E.
          Stone (ed.), *Selected Studies in Pseudepigrapha and Apocrypha, With Special
          Reference to the Armenian Tradition* (SVTP, 9; Leiden: E.J. Brill).
Thackeray, H. St. J. *et al.*
1926–77   *Josephus* (9 vols.; LCL; Cambridge, MA: Harvard University Press).
Thoma, C.
1994   'John Hyrcanus I as Seen by Josephus and Other Early Jewish Sources',
          in F. Parente and J. Sievers (eds.), *Josephus and the History of the Greco-
          Roman Period* (SPB, 41; Leiden: E.J. Brill): 127-40.
Thomas, J.
1969   'Aktuelles im Zeugnis der zwölf Väter', in Eltester 1969: 62-150.
Turdeanu, E.
1970   'Les Testaments des Douze Patriarches en slave', *JSJ* 1: 148-84.
Ulrichsen, J.H.
1991   *Die Grundschrift der Testamente der Zwölf Patriarchen: Eine Untersuchung zu
          Umfang, Inhalt und Eigenart der ursprünglichen Schrift* (Acta Universitatis
          Upsaliensis, Historia Religionum, 10; Uppsala: Almqvist & Wiksell).
VanderKam, J.
1977   *Textual and Historical Studies in Jubilees* (HSM, 14; Missoula, MT: Schol-
          ars Press).
1999   'Isaac's Blessing of Levi and His Descendants in *Jubilees* 31', in D.W.
          Parry and E. Ulrich (eds.), *The Provo International Conference on the Dead
          Sea Scrolls: Technological Innovations, New Texts, & Reformulated Issues*
          (STDJ, 30; Leiden: E.J. Brill): 497-519.

Vawter, B.
    1962   'Levitical Messianism in the New Testament', in J.L. McKenzie (ed.),
            The Bible in Current Thought (New York: Herder).

Vermes, G.
    1997   *The Complete Dead Sea Scrolls in English* (New York: Penguin Books).

Walcot, P.
    1988   'Images of the Individual', in Michael Grant and Rachel Kitzinger
            (eds.), *Civilization of the Ancient Mediterranean: Greece and Rome* (New
            York: Charles Scribner's Sons): II, 1279-90.

Wassén, C.
    1994   'The Story of Judah and Tamar in the Eyes of the Earliest Interpreters',
            Literature and Theology 8: 354-66.

Whitelam, K.
    1992   'Dan', in *ABD*, II: 10-12.

Williams, P.H.
    1980   'The Watchers in the Twelve and at Qumran', in W.E. March (ed.),
            Texts and Testaments: Critical Essays on the Bible and Early Church Fathers
            (San Antonia, TX: Trinity University): 71-92.

Winter, M.
    1994   *Das Vermächtnis Jesu und die Abschiedsworte der Väter: Gattungsgeschichtliche
            Untersuchung der Vermächtnisrede im Blick auf Joh. 13-17* (Harrisburg, PA:
            Trinity Press International).

Wise, M.
    1997   'To Know the Times and the Seasons: A Study of the Aramaic
            Chronograph 4Q559', *JSP* 15: 3-51.

van der Woude, A.S.
    1957   *Die messianischen Vorstellungen der Gemeinde von Qumran* (SSN, 3; Assen:
            Van Gorcum).

INDEXES

INDEX OF REFERENCES

BIBLE

INDEX OF AUTHORS

Guides to the Apocrypha and Pseudepigrapha

Paulson Pulikottil

TRANSMISSION OF BIBLICAL TEXTS IN QUMRAN
The Case of the Large Isaiah Scroll (1QIsaᵃ)

This book explores the nature of scribal changes in the large Isaiah scroll from Qumran (1QIsaᵃ). It offers a detailed examination of the harmonizations, explications and modernizations of the text of Isaiah by the Qumran scribe. The scribal changes in the manuscript betray his conceptual milieu and the various facets of this milieu are elaborated upon.

Pulikottil argues that those scribes who were engaged in the production of the biblical scrolls and who quoted from the biblical scrolls were not committed to a standard text. There is no evidence that the biblical scrolls copied at Qumran were made with a view to being followed by the scribe of the non-biblical texts as their standard text, but were made according to the individual notions of the scribes.

His work thus takes a new direction in the study of the biblical scrolls from Qumran, different from that of standard text-critical approaches. Biblical scrolls can be now looked at as products of creative reading of the ancient text by scribes and not just as a bundle of scribal errors.

Paulson Pulikottil is Assistant Professor in Biblical Studies at Union Biblical Seminary, Pune, India.

JSPS, 34 • 240 pp. • hb £50.00/$80.00 • ISBN 1 84127 140 3

Orders should be sent to:
Sheffield Academic Press. Mansion House, 19 Kingfield Road, Sheffield S11 9AS, England
Tel +44 (0)114 255 4433 • Fax +44 (0)114 255 4626 • email sales@sheffac.demon.co.uk

www.SheffieldAcademicPress.com

Bruce Norman Fisk

DO YOU NOT REMEMBER?

Scripture, Story and Exegesis in the Rewritten Bible of Pseudo-Philo

The Liber Antiquitatum Biblicarum, a 'rewritten Bible' that follows the broad contours of Genesis to Samuel, includes numerous secondary or out-of-sequence episodes, and frequently juxtaposes unrelated biblical characters. The subtlety and significance of these inner-biblical linkages has up to now not been fully appreciated. Building on recent studies in intertextuality, Fisk shows how Pseudo-Philo is often guided by intertextual links and themes present within the canonical precursor, that he is heavily indebted to post-biblical midrashic traditions, and that 'secondary scripture' is a strategic means by which Israel's traditions are reconfigured in this enigmatic text.

Bruce Fisk is Assistant Professor in the Department of Religious Studies at Westmont College, Santa Barbara, California.

JSPS, 37 • 376 pp. • hb £50.00/$80.00 • ISBN 1 84127 207 8

Orders should be sent to:
Sheffield Academic Press. Mansion House, 19 Kingfield Road, Sheffield S11 9AS, England
Tel +44 (0)114 255 4433 • Fax +44 (0)114 255 4626 • email sales@sheffac.demon.co.uk

www.SheffieldAcademicPress.com

*Timothy H. Lim, Hector L. MacQueen
and Calum M. Carmichael*

ON SCROLLS, ARTEFACTS AND INTELLECTUAL PROPERTY

On Scrolls, Artefacts and Intellectual Property

*edited by
Timothy H. Lim,
Hector MacQueen and
Calum Carmichael*

The Dead Sea Scrolls, found in Palestine, recovered in Jordan, largely edited by an international Christian team and possessed by the state of Israel, pose intriguing questions of legal ownership at many levels. How can modern editors claim copyright on reconstructions of ancient texts? This volume looks at international copyright and property rights as they affect archaeologists, editors and curators, focusing on the issue of 'authorship' of the Scrolls, published and unpublished.

The contributors include legal experts and many of the major figures in recent controversies, such as Hershel Shanks, John Strugnell, Geza Vermes and Emanuel Tov.

Timothy H. Lim is Reader in Hebrew and Old Testament Studies at the University of Edinburgh. Hector L. MacQueen is Professor of Private Law and Director, Shepherd and Wedderburn Centre for Research in Intellectual Property and Technology, University of Edinburgh. Calum M. Carmichael is Professor of Comparative Literature, Department of Comparative Literature and Adjunct Professor of Law, Cornell Law School, Cornell University, Ithaca, New York.

JSPS, 38 • c. 300 pp. • hb £50.00/$80.00 • ISBN 1 84127 212 4

Orders should be sent to:

Sheffield Academic Press. Mansion House, 19 Kingfield Road, Sheffield S11 9AS, England
Tel +44 (0)114 255 4433 • Fax +44 (0)114 255 4626 • email sales@sheffac.demon.co.uk

Sheffield
Academic Press

www.SheffieldAcademicPress.com

Lorenzo DiTommaso

A BIBLIOGRAPHY OF PSEUDEPIGRAPHA RESEARCH 1850–1999

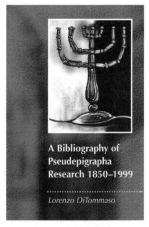

A Bibliography of
Pseudepigrapha
Research 1850–1999

Lorenzo DiTommaso

This comprehensive bibliography of research on the Pseudepigrapha and cognate literature covers the period from 1850 to the present day—thus encompassing almost all the secondary literature on this topic. A reference work designed for both institutions and individual scholars, it systematically presents a structured bibliography for each ancient text, highlighting elements such as 'Texts and Textual Issues', 'Translations', 'General Studies', and 'Specific Studies'. In addition, this book covers a host of topics related to the context and content of the classic pseudepigrapha, providing an indispensable reference tool for anyone, scholar or student, engaged on, or interested in, research in the Pseudepigrapha.

Lorenzo DiTommaso is doctoral candidate and instructor in Religious Studies, McMaster University, Canada. He has been awarded a SSHRC postdoctoral fellowship to conduct research on Daniel and the Daniel pseudepigrapha at Yale University for 2001–2003.

JSPS, 39 • c. 1067 pp. • hb £90.00/$130.00 • ISBN 1 84127 213 2

Orders should be sent to:
Sheffield Academic Press. Mansion House, 19 Kingfield Road, Sheffield S11 9AS, England
Tel +44 (0)114 255 4433 • Fax +44 (0)114 255 4626 • email sales@sheffac.demon.co.uk

Sheffield
Academic Press

www.SheffieldAcademicPress.com